Saints and Shrews

Recent Titles in
Contributions in Women's Studies

Saints and Shrews

WOMEN AND AGING
IN AMERICAN
POPULAR FILM

Karen M. Stoddard

Contributions in Women's Studies, Number 39

Greenwood Press
WESTPORT, CONNECTICUT
LONDON, ENGLAND

Library of Congress Cataloging in Publication Data

Stoddard, Karen M.
  Saints and shrews.

  (Contributions in women's studies. ISSN 0147-104X;
no. 39)
    Bibliography: p.
    Includes index.
    1. Women in moving-pictures. 2. Moving-pictures—
United States. I. Title. II. Series.
PN1995.9.W6S86 1983 791.43'09'09352042   82-15821
ISBN 0-313-23391-8 (lib. bdg.)

Library of Congress Catalog Card Number: 82-15821
ISBN: 0-313-23391-8
ISSN: 0147-104X

First published in 1983

Greenwood Press
A division of Congressional Information Service, Inc.
88 Post Road West
Westport, Connecticut 06881

Printed in the United States of America

10 9 8 7 6 5 4 3 2 1

This book is dedicated to Charlotte Bentch, who believes in me even when I find it hard to believe in myself.

CONTENTS

ACKNOWLEDGMENTS

Having read innumerable acknowledgment pages while conducting the research for this project, I am aware that there are two basic approaches to filling this page. One approach is to issue a blanket "thank you" to any individual who may have had anything to do with the final production of the text, an approach which protects the potentially faulty memory of the author and allows friends and family to assume as little or as much credit as they wish. The second approach is to list, by name, every individual who expects to be credited, a process which sometimes threatens to make the acknowledgment section a separate chapter in itself.

I have not discovered the perfect format for acknowledging the people who made significant contributions to the evolution of this book, so I have decided to use the standard Academy Award approach, in which I thank the people I absolutely could not have done the book without, and hope that everyone else understands the space limitations.

Dr. Sam Grogg, the Director of Educational Services at the American Film Institute in Washington, D.C., in the mid-1970s, suggested the topic and encouraged its development. Dr. Larry Mintz guided the original research at the University of Maryland.

The Motion Picture Division of the Library of Congress granted me extremely generous blocks of viewing time, and the staff was very helpful in suggesting supporting materials. I also made extensive use of the excellent film collection of the Prince George's Memorial Library in Adelphi, Maryland.

The College of Notre Dame provided support for clerical costs through the Pangborn Fund, as well as a place to hang my hat during the academic year.

Kathy Raab has typed more drafts than I am sure she cares to remember but remains, as always, unflappable in the face of deadlines, misspellings and anxious authors.

1

AGING:
A CULTURAL
STATE OF MIND

A woman would rather visit her own
grave than the place where she has
been young and beautiful after she
is aged and ugly.[1]

That youth goes hand in hand with beauty is as accepted a
cultural notion as the pairing of advanced age and ugliness,
particularly in respect to women and the aging process; it is
difficult to find masculine counterparts to terms such as *crone*,
witch and *hag*, each of which has the ability to call forth strong
visual images of maliciousness and degeneracy.[2]

It is only recently that the American society has begun to
awaken to the realities of an aging population. Demographic
statistics indicate that the United States in the last quarter of
the twentieth century is a graying society, a situation that is
distinctly foreign to the self-image of youthful vitality so lauded
by writers, lyricists and artists of mass popular culture. As a
culture, we do not know very much about the aging process;
our stereotypes and assumptions regarding aging overwhelmingly
reinforce negative connotations about growing older, forcing
people to anguish over a period of life that should be perceived
as part of a natural cycle rather than as an assured time of uselessness and passivity before death. To begin to comprehend the
realities of aging, it is vital to understand the origins of our

cultural beliefs, half-truths, and deceptions—to dissect the popular formulas that perpetuate cultural myths of aging—and
begin to create new standards for the cultural milieu we find
ourselves living within. This study seeks to provide such an
examination by closely investigating the images of aging women
in American popular film during the sound film era in order to
help identify the myths that were enshrined within dark movie
theatres and thus captured for all to see and share. It is not
necessarily my purpose to try to alter the myths, but rather to
interpret them for what they are and what they mean to the
culture that embraces them. It is quite a different intention to
examine myth as a means of understanding culture rather than
to examine myth with an eye toward "correcting" the myth or
the culture, as Elizabeth Janeway points out in *Man's World,
Woman's Place.* Janeway argues that myth is powerful because
it "incorporates emotions, and against these logic will not automatically prevail. . . . myth has its own, furious, inherent reason-
to-be because it is tied to desire. Prove it false a hundred times,
and it will still endure because it is true as an expression of
feeling."[3] The intention here, then, is to understand the power
of myths regarding women and aging as presented in Hollywood
movies over the past fifty years or so, "not in order 'to learn
from the past,' which is always a rather doubtful undertaking
(how do we know what it was like if we weren't there?), but
rather to remind ourselves of the enormous scope and range of
human potentiality."[4]

One well-known advertiser would have the world believe that
the aging woman is not getting older, she is getting better (rather
like a fine wine that matures with age). The initial premise of
this advertising campaign seems positive, mainly that a certain
age plateau is becoming more acceptable as an image, that a
middle-aged woman has not outlived her physical and social
usefulness. The presence of long-standing ageist stereotypes is
reflected, however, in the very fact that an advertising campaign
of this thrust and particular attitudinal nature is deemed necessary to attempt to reorient the national consciousness toward
a more positive view of the aging process (and sell a few more
bottles of hair dye or laxative or iron tonic at the same time),
helping to create new myths for the future.

If anything, the images of older women in the media are conspicuous in their absence—few magazine ads, television shows, movies, or the like, deal with the older woman specifically. Rather, the media extoll the virtues of youth, and the desirability of maintaining a youthful image as a measure of feminine fulfillment. The feminist movement notwithstanding, women in the United States are traditionally socialized to assume the roles of wife and mother at the appropriate age and to devote a significant portion of their adult lives to caring for their families. A woman's basic purpose, then, has been traditionally perceived as being biologically preordained. Since a woman's capacity, on a physical level, to bear children is relatively early in the life span, and since marriage is generally demanded as a social prerequisite to that function, women are expected to attract a marriage/sex partner at a very early stage.

Indeed, little girls no longer play exclusively with baby dolls, imitating the nurturing role of mother. Rather, observe any group of little girls with their Barbie dolls—accompanied by built-in boyfriend Ken, fabulous clothes, a townhouse and sporty car, an overly mature bustline, and no visible means of financial support—little girls imitating and mastering the role of alluring female.[5] A woman's greatest social prestige has long been associated with youth, an idealized attractiveness, and reproductive abilities; society offers few comforts or securities to the older woman who, through an inalterable physical process, no longer fits the ideal. A double standard of aging indeed exists, as Susan Sontag points out when she says, "Growing older is mainly an ordeal of the imagination—a moral disease, a social pathology—intrinsic to which is the fact that it afflicts women much more than men. It is particularly women who experience growing older with such distaste and even shame."[6]

This double standard of aging is the reason I have chosen to deal specifically with the images of aging women (rather than aging men) in popular film. It is only commonsensical to presume that images produced in a male-dominated society, within male-dominated media, will tend to reinforce and extend the power and prestige already held by the dominant group. American society, however, is too complex to be divided so neatly and simplistically into two groups based on gender;

indeed, American women are too complex to presume that they all share the same problems and aspirations. As Gerda Lerner so aptly points out, "No doubt all women are oppressed in some ways, but some are distinctly more oppressed than others."[7] Aging women, statistically, lose more in terms of social status, role definition, money, and power than aging men, and because of this multiplicity of loss, present a cultural phenomenon deserving of separate consideration. While aging women are as diverse as any other demographic group, they do share some basic characteristics as well as suffer from enough erroneous stereotypes to warrant this approach. Leila Rupp, writing about wartime propaganda aimed at women during World War II, comments, "One cannot study the experiences of women as a group, but one can study a popular conception of women, since it treats all women alike";[8] it is an approach equally appropriate to the subject of aging women.

Popular films traditionally deal with the status quo. Movies can tell a great deal about the middle and upper economic classes, but very little of the realities of the poor or minority groups; this prejudice on the part of movie studios, a result of attempting to reach the broadest movie-going audiences, is reflected within this research by the relative dearth of minority characters. The research deals with a wealth of white, middle-class women because this is the image traditionally presented within Hollywood movies.

The media cannot totally be condemned for the images they project of older women; it can be argued that images in advertising, television and films are more indicative of social attitudes and myths held by the audience toward older women. This suggests that the media operate on the basis of a few tired stereotypes (the "little old ladies with blue hair and tennis shoes getting together at the bingo game" syndrome) that are prevalent in the larger culture, or ignore the existence of older women completely. Popular media images relate to what a culture believes, wants to believe, and wishes to legitimize—these images are part truth, part myth, and part wishful thinking—and an examination of the evolving images allows speculation on their possible relationships to cultural needs and realities. A cycle exists in which the media give the audience what they feel the public wants (really meaning, what will sell to the most people while offending the smallest number of potential paying customers as possible), while the public is often highly accepting of what passes before them, the psychological strength of the media form lending instant credibility to its products. The media-produced image often takes on a larger-than-life or better-than-life sheen that is difficult for the average individual to question or compete with.

Does popular film even move significantly from its acknowledged role as reinforcer and become something a step beyond, a force of innovation and cultural change? This is a question, and a concern, that can neither be ignored nor ever answered to complete satisfaction. It is naive to insist that film commands little persuasive power; too many blatant examples of the effective use of film as a propaganda agent are to be found in Hollywood's past. The "Why We Fight" series, produced during World War II, provided both rationale and enthusiasm for the war effort; certainly, these films were reinforcing emotions already present in American society, but they are good examples of the cultural expression of a particular world view to the conscious exclusion of conflicting and/or contradicting viewpoints. Film, in this specific instance, was employed to further legitimize a political and psychological involvement which the government deemed essential to national welfare. Can it not be argued, then, that culturally expedient attitudes (such as sexism in the postwar period as a means of restoring "normalcy") could be effectively incorporated into popular entertainment within any time frame and used to help "construct" reality for the viewers? Arguments cannot be dismissed solely on the basis that they cannot be empirically proven or disproven; we must be able to assume that the art a culture produces has some connection to the guiding principles of that culture. Consequently, I accept as a guiding interpretive principle the premise that an essentially patriarchal society will produce popular culture images for a mass audience that are reflective and reinforcing of that particular social and power structure, and that the very prospect of reaching mass audiences does a great deal to help reduce our regional variations and encourage our national homogenization, helping make the

images all the more powerful and pervasive. Individuals who
doubt the power of the mass media to provide national "shared"
experiences and common understandings need only refer to
the latest movie or TV-inspired fad, from *Star Trek* dolls to
Fonzie T-shirts. As Janeway reminds us, a myth does not go
away because it is proven to be illogical; a myth or an image
finds form within a population because it speaks to desires and
wants as well as realities, forming a "reality" that is at best sub-
jective and open to manipulation. This possibility of manipulation is closely aligned to a recognition of cultural propaganda,
sanctioned by the official cultural institutions and maintained
by culturally sanctioned gatekeepers (churches, schools, media,
etc.) who have the responsibility to sift through all the pertinent data in our data-overloaded society and make some sense
of it all. Propaganda is not intended here as a term with a negative connotation (though Americans tend to believe it is something that only foreign governments engage in), but rather as
a systematic process of selective truth-telling by "official" social
and cultural agents to foster a desirable response.

Berger and Luckmann argue that the sociology of knowledge
concerns itself more with common sense than theoretical abstrac-
tions. Everyone must exist within some kind of structure, some
kind of ordered world, and people create a "reality" for themselves based on things they "know," regardless of the ultimate
validity or inaccurateness of their "knowledge."[9] This "knowledge" is taken for granted by people until, and unless, it is
directly challenged by new "knowledge." For example, the
generally accepted "knowledge" of male/female interaction in
1960 became unacceptable to the culture of 1980; a new "knowledge" had replaced the old, perhaps only substituting one set
of stereotypes for another, but definitely altering in tone. Here,
then, we find a good example of the process by which myth
assimilates new information as well as new desires and new
needs, to form new myths that are relevant to people's lives.
The sociology of knowledge is the information sought by the
popular culturist: what constructs the "knowledge" and what
meanings are attached to the various components of that shared
information?

Michael Wood notes that "entertainment is not . . . a full-scale flight from our problems . . . but rather a rearrangement of our problems into shapes which tame them, which disperse them to the margins of our attention."[10] Popular films as investigations of culture, rather than escape vehicles from culture, make more social sense; John Cawelti argues that formulaic stories strike a balance between old and new "knowledge" through the use of conventions and inventions:

> Conventions represent familiar shared images and meanings and they assert an ongoing continuity of values; inventions confront us with a new perception or meaning which we had not realized before. Conventions help maintain a culture's stability while inventions help it respond to changing circumstances and provide new information about the world.[11]

In the same vein, Hugh Dalziel Duncan sees the power of popular art as:

> the capacity to break down the walls that separate men. . . . The reveries produced by such an art as the motion picture provide us with imagery of common values, the common consummatory experiences, as well as with compensations for our defeats, our inferiorities, and our unconfessed failures.[12]

Theorists stand firmly in the assessment of film as social reinforcer, but stand back from declarations of popular film as a conspiratorial agent manipulating society to some other end. Authors who approach the subject do so carefully; anthropologist Hortense Powdermaker, speculating on the potential influence of movies on the audience, wrote: "These more or less normal everyday people may over a period of time be influenced subtly, but deeply, in their ideas of human relations, and in their values."[13] The important qualifier in Powdermaker's observation is the word "may"— it neither commits nor condemns her statement, and releases her from a potential argument that holds no absolute answers.

What can be expressed with some degree of accuracy, however, is the fact that as social ferment arises and evolves, popular film assists the culture in identifying new "knowledge" and incorporating it into the realm of accepted social meanings and functions. I acknowledge the role of popular film as reinforcer, but also firmly believe in the potential role of popular films as sources of social influence.

The cultural stereotypes society holds today regarding aging did not evolve from a vacuum. Society generally views the aging process as a series of losses—loss of friends, loss of physical abilities (blindness, deafness, lack of interest in sex), loss of mental capabilities, loss of social usefulness, and ultimately loss of self through death. While all of these conditions are possible, and the last condition certainly inevitable, the American culture focuses on the negative aspects with little regard for the potential rewards or pleasures of later life. Bowing at the throne of "newness," our culture minimizes the value of accumulated life knowledge; we do not value maturity. To be sure, our statesmen, our Supreme Court justices, and many leading businessmen are older and respected. But again, Sontag so clearly defines the situation when she says:

> "Masculinity" is identified with competence, autonomy, self-control—qualities which the disappearance of youth does not threaten. Competence in most of the activities expected from men, physical sports excepted, increases with age. "Femininity" is identified with incompetence, helplessness, passivity, noncompetitiveness, being nice. Age does not improve these qualities.[14]

The average older individual, and especially the older woman, is often treated as a burden or a social relic, someone who serves as a curiosity but has little relevance to everyday contemporary life. Elizabeth Janeway, writing as she approached the age of sixty, muses that "There's an extra bind on older women. . . . In our society we are expected to feel inferior not only as women, but also because we are old. . . . Older women here are apt to

slide down the pecking order toward a lonely old age."[15] Where
have these attitudes come from? Can any one thing be pointed
to as the instigator of our collective disenfranchisement of the
humanness of older women? The complexity of the problem
is indicative of the culture's own complex nature. American
society lives these attitudes today, but we are just beginning to
question or understand why.

The sound era of motion pictures began in 1927, and contains
several important time frames that relate to the changing roles
of women in the twentieth century. On an obvious level, the
period from 1929 to 1946 rather neatly encompasses the Depression and the American involvement in World War II. The
period was significant for women, who were to be found in
growing numbers in the work force, gaining full work participation in the war industry. The heavy movement of middle-class
women into the work world also awakened social questioning of
a so-called woman's place in American society, questioning that
not only implied that the work world made women unfeminine,
but that women in business were sounding the death knoll for
the nuclear family structure.

The Depression era was significant for the elderly; some
government recognition of their special problems came about
under the New Deal, with President Roosevelt championing
his highly controversial Social Security Act. The same period
was also significant for the motion picture industry. The advent
of sound in the late 1920s added a dimension to its entertainment potential, and the economic realities of the period forced
people to seek out inexpensive diversions in massive numbers.
Though the first years of the Depression hurt movie-going
figures, by 1936 more than 88 million Americans attended
movies on a weekly basis, that figure remaining constant until
1949 and the advent of television.[16] Indeed, only television as
we know it in our own lives has a greater potential audience on
a weekly basis than did the popular films of 1930 to 1946. To
keep that number of people returning week after week, Hollywood took few chances with its products; the movies cranked
out by the studio system, a veritable assembly line approach
to filmmaking, gave comfort and solace to an audience looking

for fantasy, for escape, for familiarity. As Andrew Bergman
states in his introduction to *We're in The Money: Depression
America and its Films*, "As films are not viewed in a void, neither
are they created in a void. Every movie is a cultural artifact—
deadly as that phrase may sound . . . and as such reflects the
values, fears, myths, and assumptions of the culture that produces it."[17] Those values, fears, myths and assumptions, as
they relate to the images of aging women, will be the focus
for attention here.

This study focuses heavily on the incidental appearances of
older women on the screen, as well as on those older characters
who are major components of a film's continuity. For purposes
of clarification, incidental roles are defined as parts which may
be extremely short in terms of on-screen time, but which are
capable of telling the careful observer an immense amount of
information about cultural attitudes and expectations. Because
of the brevity, incidental characters have very little time for
development; the audience needs to be able to relate immediately
to the significance of the action taking place involving those
characters and the progression of the plot. To accomplish this,
a director must employ "visual shorthand," broad hints to the
audience about how a particular character is to be perceived.
This shorthand, so indicative of formulaic entertainment, would
include details of physical appearance, types of activity or lack
of it, and relationships to other characters. A director can only
develop a shorthand by using accepted cultural notions, drawing
on a shared social understanding, so that the impact of the incidental character will be conveyed to the audience as strongly
as possible.[18] These somewhat fleeting images tend to be over-
looked in film analysis (and also by the audience on a conscious
level), yet because of their use by the filmmaker and acceptance
by the audience, they may be more informative in terms of cultural attitudes toward older women than the major roles regarding
aging as a theme, particularly the films of the 1960s (such as
Whatever Happened to Baby Jane?, *Wild in the Streets*, and the
like). In many instances the films of the 1960s tend to be gross
distortions of the norm and as such, misleading of the true
nature of aging, but very revealing of audience preconceptions
and social prejudices.

The films of the 1960s included in this research are those primarily of major film stars, films in which aging is the central theme. Aging seldom appeared as a major theme in the films of the 1930s and 1940s. Though there are perhaps no more than one dozen films included from this later time period, they contrast sharply with the images encountered between 1930 and 1946, and are the end result of an image degeneration of aging characters that commenced in the post-World War II period and gained full momentum some twenty years later.

Indeed, a major component of this study is my belief that the film images of older women in the late 1940s through the 1960s reflected the growing popular consciousness of the tenets of psychology, especially in the mother/child relationship. American motherhood, long held as a sacred institution, was publicly attacked in Philip Wylie's *Generation of Vipers*, published in 1942. Wylie painted a portrait of "mom" as a castrating, suffocating monster, someone who:

> is about twenty-five pounds overweight, with no
> sprint, but sharp heels and a hard backhand which
> she does not regard as a foul but a womanly defense.
> In a thousand of her there is not sex appeal enough
> to budge a hermit ten paces off a rock ledge. She
> none the less spends several thousand dollars a year
> on permanents and transformations . . . and fools
> nobody except herself. . . . But it is her man who
> worries about where to acquire the money while
> she worries only about how to spend it, so he has
> the ulcers and colitis and she has the guts of a bear;
> she can get pretty stiff before she topples.[19]

"Mom", to Wylie, was a social parasite and a source of neurotic and unhealthy children. This downgrading of Mom may have aided government efforts to recruit middle-class women for industrial work during the war, but it promised to create problems when American society looked for postwar "normality." As the war ended and the men were released from military service, some women needed to be reminded, and other women reassured, that their place was no longer in the factories (re-

ceiving money and pensions for their time), but back home
with a family to raise. Working in the home had always been
difficult, coping with children as well as household care, and
the advent of machines to relieve the drudgery had also helped
to raise the levels of boredom and restlessness of any woman
unhappily placed in the role of great American homemaker.
Middle-class women did busy themselves with childbearing
through the late 1940s and well into the 1950s, producing an
unprecedented number of children between 1947 and 1957;
43 million babies were born in that ten year boom period
(roughly one fifth of the present population), a demographic
group that promises to remain culturally dominant throughout
its lifetime, much "like a goat passing through a boa constrictor,"
according to Philip Hauser, director of the Population Research
Center at the University of Chicago.[20] During the 1950s, much
attention was focused on this demographic group. Raised by
the popular psychology of Dr. Benjamin Spock (whose advice,
supposedly, could prevent the chilling prospect of Wylie's
"Mom"), the baby boom children were the cause of America's
rush to build schools and train teachers, only to discover that
the baby "bust" brought on in the 1960s by effective contraception and legalized abortion made these efforts short-term.

The importance for this study, however, is the exaggerated
mental emphasis on youth as the most desirable life state which
gained such statistical reinforcement during the postwar period
and permeated the popular consciousness then as well as now.[21]
It is certainly of interest that the most undesirable, indeed
vicious film images of aging and aged women came about in
the 1960s, just as the baby boomers became old enough to
frequent the movie theatres on a regular basis.

In the late 1940s, two factors emerged to radically change
the audience composition for motion pictures—the 1948 Supreme
Court decision ordering studios to dispose of their company
owned theatres, and the meteoric rise of television as a means
of mass entertainment. These factors were not alone in changing
the structure of the movie industry; as Garth Jowett documents
so thoroughly in *Film: The Democratic Art*, many factors
combined in the late 1940s to hurt the movie industry, including the increase in other amusements, including professional

sports, and a "shift in expenditure patterns from amusement toward more materialistic acquisitions. . . . The motion picture was shown to be not as indispensable a part of American social life as many had thought."[22] Television was an activity that was far easier to engage in, never requiring young parents to find baby sitters for the evening or pay an admission fee beyond the initial cost of the TV set itself. Movie studios, unable to control distribution as tightly as before, cut back dramatically, abolishing the "studio system" that had mass-produced films for a weekly audience for so many years; costs were too high, and the financial risks too great, to keep stables of actors and creative personnel under long-term contracts. Weekly attendance figures plummeted, falling from 87 million in 1949 to 60 million only one year later.[23]

Television in the 1950s took on the role that motion pictures and radio had played in previous decades, that of providing entertainment to a mass audience, a task which almost assures reliance on the status quo for expressed values and moral standards, and requires the seeking out of a common denominator to unite an audience so diverse in taste, education and economic levels. As Russel Nye points out in *The Unembarrassed Muse*, "Television's most overwhelming characteristic is the size of its audience, always measured in millions, which makes it the greatest shared popular experience in history. Its life blood from the first was advertising, designed to sell products to a mass audience which in turn (as in other mass media) forced it toward conformity and standardization."[24] The TV mothers and grandmothers of the 1950s and 1960s—epitomized by Barbara Billingsley in the role of June Cleaver in *Leave It To Beaver* in her shirtwaist dress and string of pearls, baking cookies for Wally, the Beaver and their assorted buddies in her immaculate kitchen—were the women we had met in the movies of the 1930s and 1950s, transplanted intact to the small screen in America's living rooms. Movies and radio had to turn elsewhere for their audiences, eventually realizing that their new strength existed in serving specialized, rather than mass, audiences. By the mid-1960s, the first children of the baby boom era were old enough to attend movies as a social function, and the figures reveal that, indeed, the demographic bulge of people born

between 1947 and 1957 had infused new economic life into
the motion picture industry. Research conducted on an annual
basis by the Opinion Research Corporation of Princeton shows
that in the late 1960s and early 1970s, more than 75 percent of
the movie-going audience was under the age of thirty, and that
movie going increased as two variables, income and education,
rose.[25] The movies of the 1960s and 1970s, then, tend not to
be aimed at a mass market but at a very specific demographic
grouping of young, affluent, educated people who constitute
the largest demographic group in American society. This "Pepsi
Generation," doted on endlessly by the culture, believes its
own media-created image—believes that youth is the embodiment
of life, and holds primarily negative collective notions of aging
and the aging process. It is this audience that the films of the
1960s and 1970s were made for, and this audience that will,
as it grows older itself, possibly initiate a change in movie images
of aging in the opposite direction. (Indeed, as the boom children
began to enter middle age in the late 1970s, we began to see
more sensitive portrayals of the aging process, such as *An
Unmarried Woman*, *The Turning Point*, *Harry & Tonto*, Beatrice
Straight in *Network*, etc.) Television soap operas in the late
1950s and 1960s also captured the female audience that had
been the mainstay of the movie audience before and during
the war, providing most of the stronger images of women,
young or old, to be found on TV at any time.

The images of women and American sex roles as presented
in popular film have been a frequent topic for research in the
seventies; any medium so large and so much a part of the national entertainment industry for almost the entire length of
the twentieth century to date would naturally draw critical
attention in an era of feminist retrospection. Three major book-
length examinations of the images of women in film have been
published, all appearing in 1973 in the first round of books
produced directly under the influence of the most recent feminist activity in this century. The books are *Popcorn Venus:
Women, Movies and the American Dream* by Marjorie Rosen;
*From Reverence to Rape: The Treatment of Women in the
Movies* by Molly Haskell; and *Women and Their Sexuality in
the New Film* by Joan Mellen.

The tone of the three books is a collective tone of anger—
anger not only at the films, but at the social system which per-
petuated sexual stereotyping of both women and men. This
stereotyping functioned at women's expense and men's profit,
or as Rosen claims, "It was also potent escapism and a form
of popular culture so encompassing that it at once altered the
way women looked at the world and reflected how men intended
to keep it."[26] Rosen's book is, perhaps, the most vehemently
feminist, but her most glaring flaw lies in allowing her anger in
1973 to color her interpretation of films made in far different
times and cultural eras. This is a consideration Molly Haskell is
very aware of, stating "there is a danger in going too far the other
way, of grafting a modern sensibility onto the past so that all
film history becomes grist in the mills of outraged feminism.
If we see stereotypes in film, it is because stereotypes existed
in society. Too often we interpret the roles of the past in light
of liberated positions that have only recently become think-
able."[27] An example of Rosen's manipulation of the facts to
fit the theory exists in her comments regarding D. W. Griffith's
Way Down East, produced in 1920 and starring Lillian Gish as
Anna Moore. Rosen sees Griffith's treatment of the Gish character as being ruthlessly harsh—her baby dies, her phony husband
deserts her, society casts her aside—all because she was tricked
into believing that she was legitimately married. Rosen's analysis
stops at this point; she uses just enough of the story line to
support her generalization, but she neglects to deal with the end
of the film, where Anna Moore exposes the gigolo, finds real
happiness with a good man, and (most important), despite all
the horrors Rosen points to earlier in the film, survives as an
intact, stronger human being. The heroine does find happiness
in marriage in the end, but this in no way should be viewed as
a compromise of her individuality or negation of her strength.
In the cultural frame of 1920, marriage was a desirable goal.
Virginity did make a difference to the viewing audience of
1920, so that the structure of the melodrama was not as con-
trived in that social framework as we tend to judge it in retrospect. Rosen's book tells us as much about the anger and anxiety
of the early 1970s as it tells us about the history of film images
of women, and within that context makes a contribution as

one of the first serious attempts to connect media images and
socialization.

As pointed out earlier, Molly Haskell is more aware of the
necessity of placing films in the broader context of their times.
Oversimplified, Haskell's thesis is that the American film portrayal of women has gone downhill from a high point of films
in the thirties and forties showing women as strong, independent
and resourceful, to a blatant dehumanizing of and/or total exclusion of women in the films made up to 1973, with "sensitive"
males taking the roles once assigned to women. Organizing her
book chapters by decades, Haskell discerns strong images
throughout the history of popular film. She theorizes that the
demise of the studio system had a great deal to do with the
relative dearth of bankable female stars. (Rosen, too, dealt
with the studio system, but saw it as an exploitative, patriarchal
pecking order that paid more attention to breast measurements
than native acting ability. There is certainly an element of
truth in this, but Haskell's interpretation is more useful to a
broader understanding of a trend in the industry away from
female stars.) Haskell concluded that the breakdown of the
studio system, with the coinciding cut in numbers of films
produced and infrequent exposure of new actresses to the
audience, made female images harder to convey. Viewers attending a Joan Crawford film under the studio system could have
expected a particular type of woman to be portrayed *(Mildred
Pierce* jumps to mind as the model of the cynical, tough business
woman), and Haskell feels that the audience familiarity with
the star was important. Haskell also blames the breakdown of
the movie Production Code and the growing sexual license
during the 1960s for the rapidly degenerating image of women
during that same period; she indicates that the film image
changed in direct response to the loosening of rigid restrictions.
My research suggests that the changing audience demographics
during the sixties also contributed significantly to the change
in the image. Haskell did not deal specifically with the images
of older women in film, though she did observe, "As the propaganda arm of the American Dream machine, Hollywood
promoted a romantic fantasy of marital roles and conjugal
euphoria and chronically ignored the facts and fears arising

from an awareness of The End—the winding down of love,
change, divorce, depression, mutation, death itself."[28] Again,
my research argues that those same fears regarding "The End"
were a significant part of the driving force behind most of the
films of the sixties dealing with aging women.

Joan Mellen's treatment of women in film concerns itself
primarily with the 1960s and includes a great deal of analysis
of world cinema. Part of her thesis is that nationality makes
little difference, that movies throughout the world offer consistently diminished images of women, in an attempt to stop
or at least undermine awakening political consciousness among
women. She is very aware that film primarily acts as an agent of
reinforcement; she is critical of women themselves for not assuming some of the responsibility for negative screen images.
She comments that, "Victims are victims because they accept
an exploitative and alienating view of themselves. This applies
with equal force to women. To be a woman does not automatically endow insight into female experience or the distortion
of it."[29] Mellen and Haskell both call for more women to be
active in all aspects of filmmaking, behind the scene as well as
on the screen, though it would be naive to suggest that the
mere presence of women in filmmaking is any guarantee of
different images. The gender of the filmmaker is of less importance than his or her socialization. Both authors are calling for
women with raised political consciousness to involve themselves
in filmmaking, though whether the demands of the marketplace
and the ideologies of feminism can work together is a question
which is only now being approached.

A more recent examination of media images of women was
undertaken by Kathryn Weibel. Entitled *Mirror Mirror: Images
of Women Reflected in Popular Culture*, Weibel's book offers
an overview of several popular culture media as they relate to
women, including fiction, television, movies, magazines and
fashion. In her chapter dealing with film, Weibel echoes Haskell
to a large extent, crediting the thirties and forties with stronger
roles for women, and pronouncing the sixties and seventies
a veritable wasteland for images of normal, well-adjusted women.
Unfortunately, the overview approach weakens Weibel's overall
arguments. Her relatively few examples do not provide a solid,

thorough base of support for her conclusions; indeed, as one
studies her examples offered in support, one can just as easily
think of other examples to counter the argument. This, however,
is a problem inherent in the overview method, and does not
significantly discount the book. The book is valuable because
of its popular culture orientation. The various media discussed
are treated as parts of a cultural whole, not random items in a
social and cultural void. Weibel unifies her sections by citing
shared images among them, and proves a consistent pattern
of representation of femaleness in the popular culture over the
last century. She deals with trends, with cultural cause and
effect, and for this orientation the volume merits consideration.
She is very much aware that the overview approach is limiting,
saying, "This book does not aim to be a definitive study of
women in popular culture. Rather, I hope it will be a useful
and practical guide to dominant trends in the portrayal of women in popular culture and . . . suggest to each reader some of
the exciting areas of research which beckon to those interested
in uncovering and evaluating our past history as women."[30]
Weibel, in this regard, is successful. She does briefly allude to
older women in film, commenting on the roles of Bette Davis
and Joan Crawford in *Whatever Happened to Baby Jane?*, "It
is a shame that such actresses were not allowed to mature in
films by portraying the advanced wisdom which age brings,
instead of presenting aging women as freaks."[31] It is the intention of this study to discover the very answers to the obvious
questions raised by that statement.

Two particularly useful books exist regarding American films
and American culture, *Film: The Democratic Art* by Garth
Jowett and *Movie-Made America: How the Movies Changed
American Life* by Robert Sklar. Both are thorough, in-depth
works that attempt to deal with innumerable complex questions
regarding the historical structure of American movies and the
audiences they were produced for. Both studies are mammoth
in scope, but indicative of the kind of social insight that the
scholarly examination of popular films can offer. Perhaps a
book closer in scope to my study is Andrew Bergman's *We're
in the Money: Depression America and its Films*. He confines

his study to a very specific time period, commenting that "America's Great Depression was very much a stress period: not since the Civil War had one event reached into so many households and shaped so many destinies. It is a most obvious frame within which to study popular culture."[32] It is, indeed, a framework in which to examine social myths, the alteration of those myths, and how the myths were ultimately expressed in popular film as particular real events aided or impeded the social evolutionary process in the thirties and forties. So, too, does this study proceed; the image in question, that of older women, is indeed more narrow in scope than any of the books previously cited. The groundwork has already been provided by Haskell, Weibel, Sklar, Jowett and others. This study partially fulfills Weibel's suggestion that more researchers approach topics in greater depth, thus increasing and strengthening the cultural understanding of our film past and present. As Thomas Cripps, author of the excellent study of blacks in film, *Slow Fade to Black*, states in his preface, "Many of the ideas and strategies in the book stem from concepts proposed by historians and critics of popular culture for whom popular art is an expression of deep seated values and attitudes which may be studied variously as social data, collective myths, and artistic genres."[33]

The approach to the topic of older women in popular film is, in this instance, interpretive rather than quantitative. It is not enough to count the images and place them under broad categories of good or evil; the strength of this study lies in how successfully it appraises the culture and its attitudes toward aging, utilizing film as a tool for illustrating how some attitudes are articulated and altered within an artistic model.

To define "old" for this study is not an easy task, but one which must be established in some manner for the sake of general classification. Compounding the issue is the fact that "old" is different to each culture and to each time period, so that an American woman aged fifty in 1920 was considered old, while a woman of the same age in 1980 is considered middle-aged. Indeed, life expectation ranges of the various generations had a great deal to do with the definitions. As medical science keeps more people alive (and many of them generally

healthy or at least in control of their ailments) for longer peri-
ods of time than ever before in modern history, so too will the
definition of "old" be in a constant state of evolution.

Culturally speaking, women face momentous changes in their
lives directly related to the passage of time after the age of
forty-five—menopause, decrease in the full-time role of mother,
and the possibility (indeed, likelihood) of widow status can
all appear to challenge a woman's self-image, as well as the
social role assigned to her. The ways in which a woman deals
with aging related problems in her forties and fifties will have
a direct attitudinal effect on how she confronts the realities of
her sixties and seventies. Speaking directly to this concern,
psychologist Juanita H. Williams observes:

> Woman especially has always had good reasons to
> fear the passing of youth. Her most socially valued
> qualities, her ability to provide sex and attractive
> companionship, and to have children and nurture
> them, are expressed in the context of youth, which
> is endowed with physical beauty and fertility. . . .
> Since traditionally women have not been encouraged
> to develop those qualities which often improve with
> age, such as intellectual competence and the ability
> to apply mature wisdom to the solution of problems,
> it is hardly surprising that depression and feelings
> of uselessness are identified so frequently in the
> literature on older women."[34]

It is impossible, then, to pronounce an age when a woman is
"old," but it is equally impossible to perform this type of
research without arbitrarily establishing a working definition
of the term. For general purposes within this study, then,
"older women" are those over the age of fifty, though readers
should be aware that deviations from this standard may be
expected if particular films, for whatever reason, warrant an
exception.

This definition, intentionally broad in scope, attempts to
reduce the rigidity of judging aging by chronological considerations, and establish aging as a mental as well as physical process.

While I am firmly committed to the need for this approach, the very looseness of the definition may leave me open to charges of sloppy and/or convenient scholarship. Having presented my rationale for my definition, I acknowledge its potential shortcomings but am convinced of its legitimacy and utility for examining film images of women and aging over a significantly long period of time and cultural evolution.

Methodologically, the necessity of selecting films for analysis presented a large problem that could never comfortably be solved. The number of feature-length films produced for American audiences in the period under examination hovers in the thousands; selectivity is unavoidable, however, and this is not a methodological problem peculiar only to this study but to the entire range of film research. This study has focused on the holdings of the American Film Institute Collection and the United Artists Collection, housed at the Library of Congress in Washington, D. C. Though I expended almost four hundred hours of research time viewing approximately two hundred films, it is acknowledged that many other examples exist that will not be considered here.

NOTES

1. Corra May Harris, *Eve's Second Husband* (1910), quoted in Elaine Partnow, *The Quotable Woman* (New York: Anchor Books, 1978), p. 132.

2. See Mary Daly's 1978 book, *Gyn/Ecology: The Metaethics of Radical Feminism* (Boston: Beacon Press), for a full discussion of the origins and meanings of the terms *hag, crone* and *witch*. Daly meticulously establishes the inherent problems in our language of words used as sources of patriarchal reinforcement, and in our recorded history of documents that erase or ignore women's accomplishments. Daly argues effectively that words such as hag and crone, when traced to their original meanings and placed within historical context, can rightfully be interpreted as terms expressive of women whose strength and assertiveness cast them outside of the accepted realm of female behavior (as established by men), thus making them women to be both feared and derided. Daly holds that for women who understand these origins, "a Crone is one who should be an example of strength, courage and wisdom," (p. 15). While I acknowledge Daly's significant contribution to feminist scholarship in this area, the

general social attitude toward these words is still quite negative and likely to remain so for the foreseeable future.

3. Elizabeth Janeway, *Man's World, Woman's Place: A Study in Social Mythology* (New York: Dell Publishing Company, Inc., 1971), p. 28.

4. Ibid, p. 11.

5. Though, to be accurate, the "traditional" role of women as wives and mothers referred to here is relatively new, historically speaking. In *Women, Wives, Mothers* (Chicago: Aldine Publishing Company, 1975), Jessie Bernard comments that, "Motherhood as it is currently institutionalized is . . . a product of affluence. . . . And the many studies of sex-stereotyping from the primer on up have documented how insistently, almost coercively, and pervasively we have socialized girls to believe that the primary lifetime role for them was that of mother" (pp. 71-72). Carl N. Degler also thoroughly documents this relatively recent common understanding regarding the role of women in *At Odds: Women and the Family in America from the Revolution to the Present* (New York: Oxford University Press, 1980), establishing that "what today we speak of as the modern American family emerged first in the years between the American Revolution and about 1830" (p. 8).

6. Susan Sontag, "The Double Standard of Aging" (1972), reprinted in *No Longer Young: The Older Woman in America* (Ann Arbor, Michigan: The Institute of Gerontology, The University of Michigan, 1975), p. 31.

7. Gerda Lerner, *The Majority Finds its Past: Placing Women in History* (New York: Oxford University Press, 1979), p. 39.

8. Leila J. Rupp, *Mobilizing Women for War: German and American Propaganda, 1939-1945* (Princeton, New Jersey: Princeton University Press, 1978), p. 5.

9. Peter L. Berger and Thomas Luckmann, *The Social Construction of Reality* (Garden City, New York: Doubleday-Anchor, 1967), p. 15.

10. Michael Wood, *American in the Movies* (New York: Basic Books, Inc., 1975), p. 18.

11. John Cawelti, *The Six-Gun Mystique* (Bowling Green, Ohio: Bowling Green University Popular Press, n. d.), p. 28.

12. Hugh Dalziel Duncan, *Communication and Social Order* (London: Oxford University Press, 1962), p. 26.

13. Hortense Powdermaker, *Hollywood: The Dream Factory* (New York: The Universal Library—Grosset & Dunlap, 1950), pp. 11-12.

14. Ibid, p. 33.

15. Elizabeth Janeway, *Between Myth and Morning: Women Awakening* (New York: William Morrow Company, Inc., 1975), pp. 157-158.

16. Corbett Steinberg, *Reel Facts: The Movie Book of Records* (New York: Vintage Books, 1978), p. 371.

17. Andrew Bergman, *We're in the Money: Depression America and its Films* (New York: Harper Colophon Books, 1971), p. xii.

18. These distinctions of "incidental" and "major" characters are very close in spirit to the delineations made by E. M. Forster in *Aspects of the Novel* (1927) in which he defined characters as "flat" or "round" figures. Flat characters serve a purpose in novels, according to Forster, because they "are easily recognized whenever they come in—recognized by the reader's emotional eye . . . they never need introduction . . . they are easily remembered by the reader. They remain in his mind as unalterable for the reason that they were not changed by circumstances, which gives them a comforting quality." On the major, or "round," characters, Forster comments that "the test of a round character is whether it is capable of surprising in a convincing way." Certainly, flat characters are important to the novel and the popular film, not only in a structural sense—telling the story—but in a psychological reinforcement of the status quo; round characters are significant for more obvious reasons—they are the characters who bring the story to life. John Cawelti also writes extensively on the significance of stock, or conventional, characters. See *Adventure, Mystery and Romance* or *The Six-Gun Mystique.*

19. Philip Wylie, *Generation of Vipers* (New York: Farrar and Rinehart, Inc., 1942), p. 189.

20. Philip Hauser, quoted by Allan J. Mayer et al., "The Graying of America," *Newsweek*, 28 February 1977, p. 50.

21. This is not meant to imply that this cultural fascination with youth was conceived during the mid-twentieth century, for the United States has always been youth-oriented. Not only was the Republic itself youthful in the eyes of the world, but a vast psychological gulf separated the Old World of Europe from the New World of the Americas. The United States has always been youthful in fact and youthful psychologically. The first census in 1790 revealed that half the people in the country were sixteen years old or younger. Indeed, part of the collective trauma experienced by the culture now in reference to aging may be due to the beginning realization that the country is no longer adolescent in size, scope, or the eyes of the world.

22. Garth Jowett, *Film: The Democratic Art* (Boston: Little, Brown and Company, 1976), p. 344.

23. Steinberg, p. 371.

24. Russel Nye, *The Unembarrassed Muse: The Popular Arts in America* (New York: The Dial Press, 1970), p. 407.

25. Steinberg, p. 369.

26. Marjorie Rosen, *Popcorn Venus: Women, Movies and the American Dream* (New York: Avon Books, 1973), p. 19.

27. Molly Haskell, *From Reverence to Rape: The Treatment of Women*

in the Movies (New York: Holt, Rinehart and Winston, 1973), p. 30.

28. Ibid., p. 2.

29. Joan Mellen, *Women and Their Sexuality in the New Film* (New York: Dell Publishing Co., 1973), p. 52.

30. Kathryn Weibel, *Mirror Mirror: Images of Women Reflected in Popular Culture* (Garden City, New York: Anchor Press, 1977), p. xxii.

31. Ibid., p. 112.

32. Bergman, *We're in the Money*, p. xiv.

33. Thomas Cripps, *Slow Fade to Black: The Negro in American Film, 1900-1942* (New York: Oxford University Press, 1977), p. vii.

34. Juanita H. Williams, *Psychology of Women: Behavior in a Biosocial Context* (New York: W. W. Norton & Company, Inc., 1977), pp. 356-357.

2

MATERNITY AND MATRIARCHY: THE OLDER WOMAN AS MOTHER, 1930-1945

> The power of the mother has two as-
> pects: the biological potential or
> capacity to bear and nourish human
> life, and the magical power invested
> in women by men, whether in the
> form of Goddess-worship or the fear
> of being controlled and overwhelmed
> by women.[1]

The most recurring—indeed, overwhelming—image that remains
fixed in the popular film portrayals of aging women between
1930 and 1945 is that of "Mother". Mother the good, mother
the bountiful, mother the source of love and nurturance—mother flooded the middle-class audiences of the times with vivid
reminders of who she was in a cultural sense, and what society
said she stood for in the lives of all her children. It is certainly
not surprising that the film portrayal of "Mother" dominated
the representation of older women; social expectations of wom-
en preordained and reinforced the notion that biological reproduction best fulfilled women's role in the social order. What is
significant is the numbing intensity with which the image was
reiterated (almost to the exclusion of other characterizations
of older women), and the categories into which Mother fell.

Two basic manifestations of good-mother types emerged
from the popular films produced during the period of 1930

to 1945. The first manifestation was, perhaps, the most ideal-
istic, representing mothers whose very presence inspired their
truly devoted children. The relationship between this "mother
divine" and her male child was generally intense, causing him
as an adult to be righteous, successful in the eyes of the world,
and a credit to the good family name. In her study of women in
Victorian America, Ann Douglas documented the existence of
this category in Victorian literature: "The Cult of Motherhood
was nearly as sacred in mid-nineteenth-century America as the
belief in some version of democracy. Books on mothers of
famous men . . . poured from the presses; their message was
that men achieved greatness because of the instruction and
inspiration they received from their mothers."[2]

A sub-group of women existed within this category, consist-
ing of mothers whose teachings were proper and who themselves
represented goodness and virtue, but whose very goodness
caused guilt in their adult children—again, usually sons—who
strayed far from the straight and narrow path of righteous
living. This mother was often presented as an immigrant, attempting to raise her son in a culture she neither understood
nor felt a genuine part of, and was totally at a loss to help
when her boy associated with bad companions or turned to a
life of crime. She remained supportive, never condemning
her "black sheep"; the sense of right and wrong that she labored
to instill in her children eventually rose to the surface and taught
the audience the often repeated lesson that crime could never
pay (though, in the organized crime realities of the times, it
seemed to pay quite handsomely). Given the apparent fascination of movie studios with gangster and prison genre films in
the 1930s, the mother in this sub-group had many chances to
be presented on the screen.

A second category of good mothers, who appeared less frequently but loomed significantly in the lives of their children,
were the mothers who, because of death or other unavoidable
circumstances, were no longer physically present to provide
mother love. This category usually explored the resulting psychological and emotional scars that haunted the children of the
absent mother, and prevented them from functioning fully as
adults, always in search of the mothers they lost.

These manifestations of the good mother role share a common characteristic of deep and devoted love for their children. Certainly, the categories were not mutually exclusive; indeed, some films confronted motherly characters with a mixture of joy and heartache emanating from their children, the pain seemingly as welcome as the happiness, and both conditions living proof of the older woman's continuing active role as maternal agent. A mother's martyrdom appeared as a strong prerequisite to her sainthood.

A startling contrast to the varied images of the good mother was one type particularly tuned to the economic realities of the Depression era, the very wealthy matron whose head seemed stuffed with feathers rather than brains. This apparent deviation from the normally reverential attitude toward mothers, however, had more to do with social class than motherly image. Since most people in the audience could identify with financial restrictions caused by the Depression, the rich provided a safe target for satire and were presented as social pariahs, certainly not people to emulate. The scatterbrained rich mother (the idea of a scatterbrained poor woman would have been more pathetic than humorous) provided a horrendous role model for her equally spoiled children. Some strong male figure, often the disgruntled patriarch of the clan, eventually managed to restore order and some sense of stability to his household through the intercession of an outside influence (usually a poor but honest person who made the family see how ridiculous their actions were).

These different presentations of motherhood were certainly not created by Hollywood, nor were they foreign to the middle-class audiences who crowded the neighborhood theatres. If anything, the types were the result of a long-standing mother worship within the culture that had been prevalent since the mid-nineteenth century.

In their study of the historical relationship between American women and "expert" professionals, Barbara Ehrenreich and Deirdre English paint a vivid picture of the rise of the "Woman Question"—where did women belong in the Modern World?—and the romantic solution in the Victorian era that resulted in the pedestal-sitting Mother so familiar to twentieth century America.

Ehrenreich and English document American life in the late
eighteenth and early nineteenth centuries, demonstrating that
different spheres of influence did not exist as a regular part of
life in the years preceding the Industrial Revolution in this
country. While the system was patriarchal in terms of the social
power structure, women were absolutely necessary to make the
system work. Women worked on the farm, clothed the family,
and raised the children, with well-established networks of authority; women were governed by either tradition or masculine
decisions (fathers or husbands), but they had a definite place
and a definite, necessary function that meant the difference
between survival or certain death from a multitude of sources.

Ehrenreich and English cite the industrialization and capital-
ism of the nineteenth century as the causes of the shift away
from the self-contained life of family farms to a life which was
controlled by a series of interdependencies. Life rapidly divided
into different spheres, the public sphere of business governed
by men, and the private sphere of domesticity, governed, by
default, by women. The division caused many problems for
women in terms of self-image and socially assigned roles. The
factory system assumed many of the productive tasks previously
assigned to women and this removal of productive chores
caused many women to question "whether there could be any
dignity in a domestic life which no longer centered on women's
distinctive skills, but on mere biological existence."[3]

The resulting ambiguities of a social order thrown into upheaval brought many responses, both from women trying to
find a new identity and from men trying to retain a patriarchal
order that was dying in front of their very eyes. It is not surprising, in this light, that the first nationally organized stirrings
of feminism began, nor that Freud and his generation of psycho-
analysts became so engrossed in attempting to explain human
behavior.

It was necessary to encourage women to want to be in the
home and be satisfied within that particular role. Peter Gabriel
Filene, writing about the Victorian condition of American
women, pointed out: "A 'cult of the lady' held tenacious sway.
Placed upon a pedestal of piety and sensibility, she governed
the domestic half of the middle-class world while men did

economic, political and military battle beyond the doorstep."[4]
Ann Douglas elaborated on the same topic: "Praise of motherhood could bolster and promote the middle-class woman's
biological function as tantamount, if not superior, to her lost
economic productivity; imprison her within her body by glori-
fying its unique capacities . . . the cult was . . . an essential
precondition to the flattery American women were trained to
demand in place of justice and equality."[5] Mother as queen
of the house and heart could do little wrong; women were encouraged to barter away their political and social equality for
the emotional bowing and scraping of their husbands and children in front of the throne.[6]

To attack Motherhood was tantamount to attacking God,
and certainly the two were closely allied in the popular mentality. As Ehrenreich and English emphasized, women had to be
turned into the embodiment of everything the business world
was not, "The romantic construction of woman is as artificial
as the sixteen-inch waists and three-foot-wide hooped skirts
popular in mid-nineteenth century. Economic man is rational;
therefore, romantic woman is intuitive, emotional and incapable
of quantitative reasoning. Economic man is self-interested; she
is self-effacing, even masochistic."[7] Women were placed on
pedestals of moral superiority, where they were encouraged to
be submissive and obedient by elevating them to a false level
of adoration and worship. That this mentality exists even today
is strongly evidenced by the popularity of self-help books such
as *The Total Woman* by Marabel Morgan, who counsels readers:
"I do believe it is possible, however, for almost any wife to
have her husband absolutely adore her in just a few weeks'
time. She can revive romance, reestablish communication,
break down barriers, and put sizzle back into her marriage. *It
really is up to her. She has the power*"[8] (emphasis mine).

The United States government blessed mother worship by
declaring, through a joint resolution of Congress in the Spring
of 1914, that the second Sunday in May from that time on
would be known as Mother's Day, in recognition that "the
service rendered the United States by the American mother is
the greatest source of the country's strength and inspiration."[9]
The crusade to have a day set aside specifically to honor ma-

ternity was a one-woman effort by a Philadelphia resident,
Anna M. Jarvis, who conceived the idea of an international
Mother's Day, a day in which all offspring paid homage to their
maternal parent."[10] The Congressional resolution sanctified
something that the country had long recognized, that motherhood was the sacred occupation to which all women were
called, and through which women could assume their "proper"
place in American society. Jessie Bernard aptly assessed the
Victorian legacy when she wrote:

> Increasingly idealized—by definition loving, gentle,
> tender, self-sacrificing, devoted, limited in interests
> to creating a haven for her family—the mother be-
> came in time almost a parody . . . the mother adored
> for her self-abnegation . . . even her self-immolation,
> was a nineteenth-century Victorian creation. This
> image reached its heyday at the turn of the century
> and lingered on until yesterday. . . . The image still
> lurks behind the battle cry "A woman's place is in
> the home." It has retained a tenacious hold on our
> minds long after the environment that created and
> supported it has disappeared.[11]

Regardless of a mother's hold on the hearts of her children,
staying at home every day still denied women the potential
satisfaction and status of work in the business world. To counteract potential dissatisfaction with household drudgery, house-
work was elevated to the prestigious notion of "domestic science."
The change in name implied that the work involved some degree of unusual skill, ability and knowledge to be carried out
properly. But just as a custodial engineer in our own day is still
a janitor, so too was a domestic scientist still a housewife. The
title served as mere window dressing, and aided in driving any
potentially dangerous level of discontent further below the
surface of everyday life.

Middle-class women, floundering for a domestic role with
significance, again rose in national prominence in the twenties
with the rapidly developing "Age of Mass Consumption."[12] As
Thorstein Veblen so thoroughly explored in *The Theory of the*

Leisure Class, published in 1899, the notion of conspicuous consumption is a concept based on the fulfillment of irrational needs, generally satisfied through the purchase of non-essential items. The very act of purchasing goods intended to raise an individual's social status was a solid, tangible break with the pre-industrial attitude of waste not/want not frugality. Mass-produced industrial goods demanded a mass market; the economic necessities of post-World War I fostered not only the availability of manufactured goods but the easy credit means with which to obtain them. In terms of everyday consumer items, women held powerful sway over what products would be purchased, and American mass advertising was only too happy to help her make her choices. Advertising is not being blamed here for creating the need, but only cited for its enthusiasm to satisfy the desire of the buying public, and encourage the development of women as marketing agents for the products. As Goodman and Gatell observed, "Advertising trained people in new habits and values appropriate for a mass society."[13] Women were the consumers who frequented grocery stores, clothing stores, department stores, etc., and women were the people into whom advertisers wished to instill brand consciousness on the behalf of their clients. Sheila Rothman points out the dilemma of the modern woman of the early twentieth century when she writes, "Technology freed them from the menial labor that had dominated the lives of their mothers and offered them opportunities to go outside the home, but it did not free them from the commitment and obligation to the home that had structured their mothers' aspirations and choices."[14]

A socially sanctioned narcissism for women grew out of the pedestal-sitting mentality, a narcissism that gave birth to the so-called beauty industry in the twenties. The middle-class woman of the time firmly emerged as the wife companion to her husband, making "romance and sexuality central to her marriage."[15] Glamour became part of the game, an accepted preoccupation with preserving one's physical appearances and, at the same time, helping to satisfy the national economic necessity of consumer spending. Middle-class women in the twenties, then, reassumed a vital role in making the system work by becoming the buying force of the consumer culture, a role that continues some sixty years later.

The popular films of the thirties were not the only mass
entertainment force to deal heavily with the multivaried images
of "mother." Radio network soap operas, born in the thirties
to sell soap powders to the house-bound women of America,
carefully reinforced positive maternal images for the predomi-
nant listening audience of young and middle-aged women. In
almost all soap operas, the basic setting centers on home life
and the various, complicated interpersonal relationships of the
major characters. Soaps fall short of depicting real life, as countless critics have pointed out, but their intention is more geared
toward providing a degree of fantasy life for the audience, not
imitating the humdrum of everyday routine. Characters are
well developed psychologically—much more than film or prime
time television characters—principally because the daily doses
of soaps provide enough time to explore people and situations
in depth. On the other hand, to strike a responsive chord in as
many members of the audience as possible, the characters often
revert to a type. The title character of the radio soap, *Ma Perkins*, was an elderly woman described as a "helping hand, deeply
concerned about the lives of others, but with little dramatic
life of her own."[16] Ma was a trusted confidante and a veritable
fountain of wisdom from which misguided and confused young
people could draw a large measure of direction and inspiration.
Soap mothers tended to be self-sacrificing, centering their energies on their offspring. Another soap mom, widowed Mother
Dawson, was asked by her teenage daughter why she never
married again; Mother Dawson replied that "I was too busy
bringing up two babies to be intrigued by anything but sewing
and mending and washing and ironing."[17] Soap mothers seemed
to have few interests that took them beyond their own front
yards. Another radio soap character, Young Widder Brown
(from the show of the same name), could not bring herself to
remarry without the complete approval of her children. The
soap itself was introduced as "the conflict between a mother's
duty and a woman's heart,"[18] as if the two were mutually
exclusive. *The Goldbergs*, created by Gertrude Berg as a radio
soap, was a durable thirties ethnic depiction of Jewish mothers
(long before Mrs. Portnoy made her appearance) with the typical devotion to children and husband.[19] The powerful pre-

sence of Molly Goldberg totally dominated the world in which
she lived, indeed the world she created and nurtured with tireless
effort. The list of faithful, devoted mothers goes on and on, so
that soap mothers served an important social function in the
thirties, providing a safe and stable haven for their husbands
from the harsh realities of the work world, and creating a nurturing environment that would produce somewhat confused
but well-intentioned children who would always need their
mothers. Mother would always be around to support and love
her children—it was the reason she existed.

Women's magazines and pulp stories of the "true romance"
and "true confession" variety also proliferated during the thirties, reinforcing the maternal ideal for the millions of impressionable readers who mentally inhaled the thinly disguised
lessons. As Nye points out, "The message of the love-pulp to
girls was work, wait, discriminate, keep control, and you should
someday find security, stability, and possible 'romance'. . . .
Love pulps dealt almost wholly with courtship, ending in marriage or the guarantee thereof."[20]

That movie-going in the twenties and thirties was an elaborate
cultural ritual has been well documented by Jowett and Sklar
in their respective works dealing with American film; that
movie-going in that same time period was quite close to a secular
religious experience, an almost total suspension of reality in
surroundings and film content, can be documented by the
elaborate and ostentatious movie palaces that sprang up in
every decent sized city in the country. To a contemporary
movie-going audience reduced to viewing current films in multi-
unit cinemas that more resemble the storefront theatres of the
early silent era (featuring paper-thin walls, Munchkin-size screens,
inaudible sound systems, and reheated popcorn), the size and
grandeur of the old movie palaces may appear an exercise in
overkill—an unnecessary and pompous display of misplaced
values and expectations. The fantasy, escapist world on the
screen, however, was made all the more fantastic by the cathedral-
like surroundings of theatres such as The Rialto ("Temple of the
Motion Picture") in New York, the Paramount on Times Square,
the Roxy, and many others of equal fame. These movie palaces
employed the visible signs of grandeur—the crystal chandeliers,

the corps of uniformed ushers, the white-gloved projectionists, washroom fixtures made of solid gold, the incredibly ornate architectural styles—and the images on the screen, looming over all, became objects to be adored and sanctified. Ben M. Hall spoke of the effect of the movie palace on the people it was intended to attract:

> The people loved it. After all, it was for them that this sumptuous and magic world was built, and they thoroughly enjoyed being spoiled by indulgent impresarios. Ladies from the cold-water flats could drop in at the movie palace after a tough day in the bargain basements and become queens to command. Budgets and bunions were forgotten as noses were powdered in boites de poudre worthy of the Pompadour. From a telephone booth designed as a sedan chair, Mama could call home and say she'd be a little late and don't let the stew boil over.[21]

Just as the great cathedrals of Europe were built when the people were much more devoted to their religious life, so too were the movie palaces built during a time when people were much more serious about their movie-going, when the act of "going to the movies" had far more significance as an experience than it does today. These movie palaces were certainly right and proper places to worship "Mom," to speak of her in hushed and reverential tones.

A movie "mother" of the first type—someone loyal, true and inspiring—need not necessarily be the natural mother of the character in question. The maternal role in film during this period was generally assumed to be part of an older woman's innate character, not only the result of biological function, so that some mothers discussed here may actually be aunts or older friends or particularly important people in a character's life, performing in a motherly capacity.

Many older actresses played a succession of mother-like roles, building a screen image for themselves that allowed audiences an intimate expectation each time they appeared in a film; Beryl Mercer was one of these women, a British character

actress who started her Hollywood career in 1923.[22] Her role
as Ma Powers in *Public Enemy* (1931) was the personification
of unquestioning maternal love. Ma Powers had two sons, trouble-
maker Tom (James Cagney) and reliable Mike (Donald Cook),
but she loved each without making distinctions because of their
activities; the Cain and Abel motif, as well as the Prodigal Son
resemblance, worked effectively as the basis for this stock
situation. Tom falls in with bad company, turning to a life of
crime; Mike works hard for a living, supporting his mother,
and worrying about his brother. Faced with a realization of
Tom's activities, Mike comments, "The worst part of it all is
that he's lying to his mother," concerned that the all-important
mother/child relationship is being violated. Tom's mob connections lead ultimately to his murder by other mobsters, his
body being delivered to his mother's front door, shakily prop-
ped so as to fall across the threshold as the door is opened. The
discrepancies in the behavior of the two sons never shake Ma
Powers' belief in, or love for, either of them, pressing home to
the audience that a mother's love is total, complete and non-
judgmental. Her reward, meager though it is, comes at the end
of the film when Tom, dying, says "I ain't so tough" and his
facade of evil dissipates as he pays for his wrongdoing with his
life. By the conclusion of the film, the audience learns that
toughness is fleeting, crime does not pay, and a boy can always
go home to his mother.

Mercer's role is particularly troubling because her character
is so thoroughly helpless to alter the fate of her children; the
moral superiority and power presumed for all women is impotent
for the immigrant mother. A close analysis of the character of
Ma Powers may well suggest that the power of the pedestal
diminished for women whose backgrounds moved them far
away from the middle-class, WASPish ideal; Ma, an aging immigrant, could only stand by and watch the disintegration of
her family within a culture of which she could never truly be
a part. Ultimately, the "power" held by all women (WASPs as
well as immigrants) by virtue of gender was a carefully constructed facade, designed to enclose an illusion that had no
true counterpart in reality.

Another Beryl Mercer performance in 1931 occurred in a

vehicle for Barbara Stanwyck titled *The Miracle Woman*. A
Frank Capra film, it concerns the story of a dishonest woman
evangelist (interestingly enough, with no mother to guide her),
bitter about the abusive treatment her minister father received
from his well-to-do congregation after many years of faithful
service, and determined to achieve some measure of revenge
against the Christian establishment by bilking gullible people
who believe in miracle cures. John Carson (David Manners), a
blind songwriter, lives in elderly Mrs. Higgins' (Beryl Mercer)
boarding house; Mrs. Higgins is fond of John and cares for
him—bringing him dinner, reading his mail to him, etc.—since
his blindness is of rather recent origin and his orientation to
his disability is incomplete. Discouraged over his inability to
sell any songs, John is deeply depressed until he hears, by chance,
a radio broadcast by Sister Florence Fallon (Stanwyck) exhort-
ing people to live up to their capabilities. Inspired, John and
Mrs. Higgins attend a Fallon revival, which approximates a
three ring circus, complete with cages of lions on stage to be
tempted by delectable Christians. Florence's ability to walk
inside the cage without being attacked is suggestive of her own
predatory nature; she is more allied in spirit with the lions than
with the people in the audience who came to be helped. Ultimately meeting and falling in love with John causes Florence
to want to redefine her goals and aspirations, with Mrs. Higgins
leading the cheering squad for Florence's transformation. John
and Mrs. Higgins are simplistic people, but honest and direct.
Florence is portrayed as an intelligent but bitter young woman
who is shown the road to righteousness not by her own ministry
but by the goodness of John and his landlady. When she appears on stage in her "Tabernacle of Holiness" to confess her
sins, the lights short-circuit and burn the church to the ground.
Six months later, we find Florence loving John and singing with
a Salvation Army street band, a far less glamorous but singu-
larly more rewarding existence. As the opening statement of the
film cautioned, *"The Miracle Woman* is offered as a rebuke to
anyone who, under the cloak of Religion, seeks to sell for gold,
God's greatest gift to Humanity . . . Faith." Indeed, it is the
simple but firm faith of John and Mrs. Higgins that saves Florence and restores her to a true Christian perspective; Mrs. Hig-

gins serves as a moral yardstick, a standard by which the younger
characters are able to measure their own growth.

A third example of Mercer's expertise at playing mothers
is exhibited in the 1934 RKO film, *The Little Minister*, in which
she played the role of Margaret Dishart, mother of Gavin Dishart, a young minister of small physical stature but larger-than-
life spiritual presence. The film is not just of interest for Mercer's
role, but for the comparison/contrast between Margaret and
another old character, Nanny (Mary Gordon). Gavin, newly
ordained, is appointed to his first church and brings his mother
with him to be mistress of his home. Margaret has obviously
been a large source of inspiration and support, and Gavin's
ministry is a reward for both of them. Set in a Scottish weaving
town in 1840, part of the story revolves around conflicts between
the mill workers and the company owners, a topic that union-
minded audiences of 1934 could certainly appreciate. A young
girl, Babbie (Katharine Hepburn), is a mysterious person who
dresses like a gypsy (considered outcasts by the townspeople)
and is sympathetic to the plight of the townspeople, providing
pertinent information to the mill workers to aid their revolt.
As the story unfolds, she is in actuality the legal ward and soon-
to-be bride of the mill owner; she is rich but believes in the rights
of the poor, a perfect embodiment of New Deal sensitivity. In
the story, an old woman called Nanny is no longer able to
support herself and is told she must go to the poor house.
Miserable about having to leave her home of so many years,
her income is guaranteed by Babbie's intercession and the two
women become close friends. Babbie and Gavin fall in love,
but circumstances stand in their way. Nanny, however, prays
to God, saying, "Oh, Lord, you can't mean for them to bury
their youth so soon. Look at me. What is anything when you're
old without somebody?" The lesson is only too clear; an old
age spent alone is an empty life, an existence without merit or
purpose. Contrasted with the satisfaction Margaret finds in
Gavin's mission, Nanny's life is dim because of her lack of
husband and children. The necessity of traditional family ties
is borne out as a prerequisite to life satisfaction for women.
When the two lovers finally reconcile their differences, Babbie
worries that their backgrounds are too diverse, that Margaret

will not accept her. In a genuine self-sacrificing maternal response
to Babbie's dilemma, Margaret reassures her that, "Gavin will
tell you, my prayers have ever been for his happiness; in that
I will see my own." A mother living not only for her children,
but vicariously through her children, is a theme often repeated
during the films of the thirties. This slavish devotion to the welfare of children both reinforced and validated the cultural image
of women as mothers. The economy of the thirties had difficulty keeping men employed, let alone encouraging women to remain in or enter the work force; the duties of maintaining a
home and raising children provided women with a culturally
sanctioned role and purpose, something the Depression economy
was unable to do. The total absorption of women by motherhood ultimately reduced the importance of women as individuals
with personal goals and aspirations unrelated to the nurturing
of others, a denial of the self which women in the eighties are
still struggling to overcome.

Another Frank Capra film, *Lady for a Day* (1933), starred
May Robson as Apple Annie. This film was successfully remade
by Capra in 1961 as *Pocketful of Miracles* and starred Bette
Davis in one of her few "respectable" older women roles; the
two versions are quite similar. The story is of the Cinderella
variety, but with a twist—the woman is not young and beautiful
and married to a prince, but rather an elderly panhandler in
New York City who has slaved for years in order to be able to
support her illegitimate daughter in a stylish Spanish convent
school. Annie allows her daughter to believe she is wealthy,
posing as a rich dowager who writes daughter Louise letters on
the fancy stationary of a famous hotel. It is obvious Annie is
educated—she listens to classical music while writing eloquent
letters to her daughter—but the audience is left to speculate as
to how she managed to end up living in a one room dump,
ruining her kidneys with too much gin, and begging for a living.
Annie is obviously resourceful, managing to keep Louise in
school for eighteen years, but Louise sends word she is coming
to America to introduce her fiance, a Spanish nobleman. Apple
Annie is distraught; her farce is in danger of being exposed,
and she considers suicide. Her friend, Dave the Dude, a gangster
with a soft heart and a superstition that Annie's apples bring

him luck, sets Annie up in a penthouse apartment, hires a team of cosmetic technicians to transform her (causing the Dude's chauffeur to exclaim, "She looks like a cock-a-roach that turned into a butterfly"), and helps Annie convince Louise that her mother is, indeed, Mrs. E. Worthington Manville, leader of New York society. The playacting over, Louise returns happily to Spain and Annie's limousine turns back into an apple cart as she once again plies her trade. Annie had said at one point that "ever since Louise was born, I have lived for one thing—her future" and yet Louise's future excluded any kind of decent life for Annie. Even though her child had always lived several thousand miles away from her, Annie's total focus was her daughter and what she identified as her responsibility to Louise. The daughter, by Annie's own account, had been illegitimate—was Annie's lifestyle a punishment for transgressing acceptable social standards? Must mothers suspend all self-interest in the pursuit of happiness for their children? Indeed, are mothers responsible for making their children happy? All of these questions received a resounding "yes" in reply in the typical Hollywood product of the thirties. Annie returns to selling her apples with gusto, not complaining or self-pitying, but self-sacrificing to the end.

The 1935 production of *Roberta* starred Helen Westley in the title role as an elderly but renowned dress designer in Paris whose roots are firmly embedded in Indiana, where she is still known as Minnie. Stephanie (Irene Dunne) is a secretary, companion, and design partner to Roberta, caring for her much like a daughter. Roberta is a woman who dresses regally, but possesses a finely tuned sense of humor and a very down to earth approach to life. Roberta's nephew, John (Randolph Scott, of cowboy fame), arrives in Paris, where Roberta tries to shake a little of the farm dust out of his hair by taking him to a good tailor and hiring a French tutor, as well as encouraging John's romantic interest in Stephanie. Roberta's role is cut short by her death during her regular afternoon nap, but her mothering regard for both Stephanie and John carries through the remainder of the film. John inherits the shop, but realizes that his aunt would have wanted Stephanie to have it; she agrees to enter into a partnership with him. Eventually, after a series of misunder-

standings, Stephanie and John are married. Roberta obviously
served as a foil for John's developing relationship with Stephanie,
but otherwise served little purpose to the film in and of herself.
She is dead by the end of the first hour of footage and, as it
turns out, Roberta had not designed any of the clothes bearing
her name and label for several years due to her failing health.
Stephanie was Roberta, or at least the Roberta the fashion
world admired, and she kept the secret out of her loyalty to
the woman who had treated her so well. The message from this
film is somewhat different, namely that a good and generous
attitude will be rewarded by the love and devotion of one's
"children." At the point in life when the audience meets Roberta, she has little function, little purpose, and yet is a positive
characterization. Perhaps the devotion displayed by Stephanie
is to be interpreted as a just reward for her benefactor, a reward
that generous parents in the audience could reasonably expect
from their children. Again, family structure reasserts its importance and desirability for the thirties audience.

A C & C Films production in 1938, *Mother Carey's Chickens*,
presented a familiar portrait of mother love and perseverance
in the midst of seemingly insurmountable odds. Three older
women characters appear, one of whom is Fay Bainter as Margaret Carey, widow of a poor naval captain and mother to four
children. For years, the Carey family had travelled all over the
country to be with Captain Carey, a gregarious family man; as
the children grew into adolescence, however, they longed for
a greater sense of stability. The opening line of the film informed
the audience, "This story is about one of the countless families
who move from place to place, always seeking and longing for
a home." Daughter Katherine (Ruby Keeler) chides her father in
the beginning that "Regular families stay put, and have fathers
who come home at night." When Captain Carey is killed in the
Spanish-American War, Mrs. Carey becomes not only the emotional support of her children, but the financial support as well;
she goes to work in a textile mill to supplement the meager
government pension she receives each month. An industrial
accident (in which she is nearly maimed) marks the end of
Margaret's factory career, and the family's financial condition
seems in bleak and dire straits. Captain Carey's only living

relative was his Aunt Bertha (Alma Krueger), a rich, matronly
and unemotional spinster. Aunt Bertha offered to take two
of the older children and allow them to live with her in Mas-
sachusetts while receiving their education; she informs the children that they will be allowed to visit Margaret once each year.
Margaret stoically encourages the children to accept Bertha's
offer, knowing she cannot provide them with the type of education her husband would have desired. The children refuse
the gesture, deciding not to leave the family, and Bertha (totally
unable to comprehend their loyalty and love for Margaret)
washes her hands of the entire situation. We never encounter
Aunt Bertha again, but her childless existence is clearly presented
as a reminder of what awaits a woman who does not develop
her motherly instincts—a later life of unhappiness and loneliness
that no amount of money can alter.

   To support themselves, the Careys rent and restore an immense Colonial mansion and start a boarding house for local
teachers. The house had stood vacant for years, but the family
enthusiasm and love brought it back to life. At this point,
another aging woman, Mrs. Fuller (played by Margaret Hamilton—currently spokeswoman for Maxwell House coffee as the
self-assured Cora—who always looked twenty years older than
she actually was), a rich woman who totally dominates her
husband, sees the house and schemes to buy it and evict the
Careys. Mrs. Fuller dresses severely—all in black—and has a
personality to match her wardrobe. Aided by friends, the Careys
gather forces to counteract the Fullers, successfully convincing
Mrs. Fuller the house is haunted. The purchase deal quickly
falls through and the family retains the home they had waited
so long and patiently to have. The rich people in this film, Aunt
Bertha and Mrs. Fuller, are insensitive and unfair, quite sure
that their money supersedes all other ethical and moral considerations. As older women, these two negative characters
certainly help Margaret Carey appear all the more saintly. With
little in their favor other than familial solidarity, a strong mother,
and good friends, the Careys triumph over the rich by employ-
ing their wits and drawing on their emotional strength. *Mrs.
Carey's Chickens* is a perfect Depression era film; indeed, the
story is universal in American popular entertainment, "proving"

that righteousness and honor always prevail in the presence of insensitive power and the misuse of money.

The John Ford film *Young Mr. Lincoln* (1939) dealt with a very short period in Abraham Lincoln's life, his time as a young lawyer in Illinois, long before his rise to regional and national prominence. Lincoln (Henry Fonda) is engaged as the defense attorney for the Clay brothers, two young men accused of murder. Their mother, Abigail Clay (Alice Brady), is portrayed as loving, protective and kind, a definite peacemaker; Mrs. Clay's goodness is further brought home by Lincoln's affection for her. He tells Mrs. Clay that his mother, Nancy Hanks, would have been about Mrs. Clay's age if she had lived, and a lot like her—a mother of goodness and faithfulness. Mrs. Clay was the only eyewitness to a fight her sons engaged in with the murder victim, and as such was called to testify against them at the trial. She refuses to name either son as the murderer, saying it would be like choosing between them. Mr. Lincoln, outraged at the prosecutor's berating of Mrs. Clay, verbally rises to her defense, saying, "Mrs. Clay is one of those women who say little and do much, who ask for nothing and give all, and I tell you that such a woman will never answer the question that has been put to her here. Never." Lincoln's defense stands not only as a defense of Mrs. Clay, but a defense of the assumed prerogatives of motherhood; indeed, his assessment could well stand as the definition for this broad category of "loving Mother." Mrs. Clay's faith in her sons was borne out when Lincoln managed to reveal the identity of the real murderer, who had stabbed the victim after the original fight was over. Her devotion in the presence of damning circumstantial evidence kept her sons from an early hanging, and suggested that maternal intuition is a force not to be doubted. It is not too difficult to see how the Lincoln mythology grew and prospered in this country; certainly, his homely, folksy but honest presence was a characterization properly suited to Depression era retelling, particularly when coupled with a defense of a frontier mother's self-sacrificing love for her children.

The 1939 production of *The Wizard of Oz* provided three specific images of aging women, two virtuous and one evil. Dorothy Gale is a young girl living on a drab Kansas farm,

yearning for a more adventurous life "over the rainbow." An
accommodating tornado sends her to the Land of Oz, a colorful
but bewildering place that Dorothy instantly sets about trying
to leave. The movie is the story of Dorothy's pilgrimage back
to Kansas, with all the problems she encounters along the way.

The most important older woman in *The Wizard of Oz* is
Auntie Em, played by Clara Blandick. Her role was not considered all that important by filmmakers, evidently, since her
credit was listed below even that of Toto, Dorothy's dog. In
all actuality, however, Auntie Em is Dorothy's guiding force
throughout the story. The audience's first glimpse of Em is in
a crisis situation, attempting to save baby chicks threatened by
a broken incubator—a very maternal role, substituting for the
real mother the chicks were denied. Auntie Em is not portrayed
as a particularly affectionate person, but we know through
other means that she is a good woman who is concerned with
the welfare of others.

Dorothy's initial crisis stems from her dog's penchant for
chasing a cat owned by Elvira Gulch (Margaret Hamilton). Miss
Gulch, rich and unmarried with a face that could halt time,
insists on having Toto destroyed because he bit her while she
was defending her cat. To save Toto, Dorothy runs away from
home, decides to go back after Professor Marvel convinces her
Aunt Em is ill, and gets knocked unconscious when she returns
to the farm in the midst of a tornado. In Dorothy's subsequent
dream world, Auntie Em is the only supporting character (be-
sides Toto) who appears in the fantasy world as herself; the
hired hands become the Scarecrow, the Tinman and the Cowardly
Lion, Professor Marvel becomes the Wizard of Oz, and Elvira
Gulch becomes the Wicked Witch of the West, a classic representation of the evil hag who preys on innocent children.

It is the image of Auntie Em that leads Dorothy through
her incredible journey, longing for the security, comfort and
stability of Kansas as represented by the drab, graying presence
of Auntie Em. Sent off by the Wizard to kill the Witch of the
West, Dorothy is captured and made a prisoner in the witch's
castle for refusing to surrender the magical ruby slippers. Imprisoned, and with time running out, Dorothy calls out in desperation to Auntie Em, whose image appears in the witch's

crystal ball. Dorothy tells Auntie Em that she is trying to get
home to her, but the image fades and is replaced by the grotesque
face of the witch, mocking Dorothy's calls for help.

Dorothy's arrival in Munchkinland launched her experience
in the unpredictable land. Her house fell on the Witch of the
East, killing her, and made Dorothy a heroine to the Munchkins but an enemy to the Witch of the West. The ruby slippers—
red, sparkling and bright, representative of youth and vitality—
are in stark contrast to the green skin and black robes of the
Witch who covets them. Throughout the ordeal in Oz, the
Wicked Witch establishes roadblocks in Dorothy's pursuit of
home, for which Auntie Em is the constant symbol. Indeed,
the Wicked Witch's relationship to Dorothy is entirely com-
posed of trying to kill her—to obtain the power of the ruby
slippers, to assert the power of age and evil over youth and
goodness, and to symbolically and practically rid herself of the
threat of competition Dorothy's youth represents. Miss Gulch
and the Wicked Witch together represent the potential "other
side" of an older woman's personality—the side which seems
to grow from a self-centered, childless existence—and act as a
reminder to all about the unhappy outcome of women who do
not fulfill their maternal destinies.

The third older woman character is Glinda, the Good Witch
of the North, protrayed by Billie Burke. Glinda's main function
is to act as the protectress of the Munchkins, a beautiful sparkling witch who sails into Munchkinland as a ball of light, as
compared to the Witch of the West, who emerges from choking
clouds of black smoke. The contrast between Glinda and the
Witch of the West illustrates the basic conflict between "good"
older women and "evil" older women. Billie Burke was fifty-four
years old when she portrayed Glinda, yet her physical appearance is that of a much younger woman, accentuated by her
glittering gown and flowing blonde hair. Glinda's appearance
is in stark contrast to the plain but dismal image of Margaret
Hamilton's green skin, overly sharp facial features and traditional witch's garb. Glinda's voice is soft and soothing, while the
Witch's voice is shrill and menacing. The Wicked Witch is even
denied the basic human identification of a name. Throughout
the film, she is known only as the Wicked Witch of the West

(a fate shared by her unfortunate sister, the Wicked Witch of the East), while the Good Witch of the North has the distinction of the somewhat lyrical name, Glinda.

The depiction of a witch as "good" is unique for the twentieth century, particularly within popular culture images; Dorothy, upon meeting Glinda, is perplexed by Glinda's self-description, insisting that witches are "old and mean and ugly." Glinda is, in many ways, a reminder of the pre-sixteenth century European distinctions of "good" witches as wise and powerful women who possess magical healing powers.[23] When *The Wizard of Oz* was released in 1939, however, the viewing audience clearly understood witches within the modern context to be evil and destructive women, the "shadow and opposite of the loving mother. . . . The witch, in short, is the bad mother."[24] The seeming contradiction of Glinda as a good witch who helped people was merely another way in which the Land of Oz was so different from the reality of Kansas. Glinda is, without doubt, the loving mother to Dorothy. Glinda sets Dorothy off in pursuit of the Wizard of Oz. She guides Dorothy, but does not attempt to control her or tell her what to do; Glinda allows Dorothy to make her own mistakes and discover her own values. In that sense, she is the perfect Mother—protecting her child but also allowing her to grow up on her own terms.

Dorothy's inadvertent but effective liquidation of the Wicked Witch points even more conclusively to the miserable fate of older women who do not nurture others, particularly children. No one, not even the soldiers who served her, mourns the death of the Wicked Witch; the soldiers hail Dorothy as a heroine who has released them from the Witch's power, and present Dorothy with the Witch's broom as a trophy of her triumph—a triumph of youthful innocence over aged wickedness.

Dorothy's release from the Wicked Witch does not help her return to Kansas, for the Wizard did not really have the power to effect such a miracle; as he said, "I'm a very good man—just a very bad wizard." Glinda saves the day, telling Dorothy she always had the ability to get home but that she needed to learn the fact for herself. Dorothy thinks about what her experience has taught her, and pronounces a lesson that only confirmed what people had long suspected—that the grass is al-

ways greener on the other side of the fence, but often turns
out to be crabgrass on closer examination. As Dorothy explains,
"If I ever go looking for my heart's desire again, I won't look
any further than my own backyard, because if it isn't there,
I never really lost it to begin with," an approach the political
isolationists of the late thirties would have appreciated. Dorothy
pronounced what a whole society already accepted as truth,
that a woman's place (and a woman's true happiness) was at
home.

In *The Wizard of Oz*, the good solid values of Kansas, where
everything is black and white and people can be sure of what
they see and what they know, is far preferable to the enchant-
ing but confusing and phony world of Oz. Even the leader of
Oz, the Wizard, is not what he pretends to be. He gets along
with the populace by a show of hollow power, with lofty speeches
that instill false confidence in his rule, and a particular talent
for hiding his weaknesses. As Wizard, he was full of hot air, as
symbolized by his career as a state fair balloonist. The symbolic
presentation, and mistrust, of Roosevelt's New Deal socialism
as seen by some segments of the audience, cannot be discounted
in this late thirties fantasy for movie-goers of all ages.[25]

Political concerns, indeed, came into greater prominence as
potential movie subject matter toward the close of the thirties.
With few exceptions *(I Am a Fugitive from a Chain Gang* and
Our Daily Bread among them), American popular film during
the Depression existed almost totally outside the realm of current events—little attention was paid to unemployed veterans,
hungry families, or themes likely to depress the general public.
Reality had little to recommend it in the thirties, on a national
or international level. As the forties dawned, however, and the
Depression was rapidly evaporating in an atmosphere of war-
related industrial growth and renewed prosperity, Hollywood
(and, perhaps, its audience) seemed somewhat better equipped
to deal with the hardships and inequalities of the preceding
ten years, and the uncertainties of the near future. "Mother
divine" safely weathered the transition in approach and story
line, proving the durability of the symbolic mother as a rallying
point in good times as well as bad. The image of mother became even more important as the American entry into World

War II drew closer to reality; mother was a sentimental rationalization for patriotism and an added incentive to fight to
protect and preserve all she represented. Leila Rupp points
out, "On the eve of the Second World War, the ideal woman . . .
was above all a mother with duties and functions radiating
from this central role."[26] This "central role" of mothering
would face unique challenges in the forties.

In 1940, John Ford directed *The Grapes of Wrath*, starring
Henry Fonda as hothead Tom Joad, and Jane Darwell as Tom's
ever-optimistic mother, Ma Joad (a role which won her an
Academy Award for Best Supporting Actress). The Joads are
Okies, sharecroppers in Oklahoma during the thirties who are
forced off their land by the owners. They decide to head for
California and the promise of jobs. Tom Joad returns from
prison (having served four years for manslaughter) just in time
to join his family on their journey. Ma's first concern upon seeing Tom is whether or not prison made him "mean and bad,"
but he denies both. Ma's indomitable spirit first peeks through
as the family, possessions haphazardly balanced on their old
truck, sets off. One son encourages Ma to look back, but she
refuses, saying, "We're going to California, aren't we? Then let's
go to California." Ma had left behind almost everything she
had ever known or loved, but she would only allow herself to
look forward and hope, not look back and regret; no society
could ask for a stronger role model for its citizens.

Grandma and Grandpa Joad both die on route to California,
as if that new land of promise had no place for people so obviously a part of another place and time. The Joads begin to
hear that California is not the oasis they think it is, but they
have nowhere else to go, and so they push on. As soon as the
family crosses the California border, they stop and bathe in a
river—the symbolic baptism into the land of promise. Forced
to camp in an ill-run and filthy transient camp, the Joads initially find nothing but misery and human suffering; people
want to work but are exploited by employers who pay little
better than slave wages. Again, Ma does her best to rescue the
situation by trying to feed not only her family, but stretching
their meager rations into a stew she shares with wide-eyed,
hungry children living in the camp.

Tom becomes incensed at the treatment he sees people receive, but Ma reminds him that he promised to control his temper for the good of the family. The importance of the family is a prevailing theme in this film; family solidarity is Ma's main concern. Her ideas about family are also closely aligned to the importance of the land and the importance of belonging someplace. The land provides boundaries for the family; without the boundaries, the family unit faces the possibility of disintegration. As Ma says, "Without the land, there's nothing to trust."

Tom gets into trouble killing a guard at a ranch in self-defense. He knows he must leave, but Ma insists that they all leave together, that Tom help her hold on to whatever is left of their family. The Joads stumble, providentially, into a government-operated camp with running water, bathrooms, and cabins—a veritable paradise compared to their earlier experiences. The camp is run by committees elected from among the campers, with strong hints of the positive aspects of communal living. Ma is very happy at the camp, where she has not only a clean and decent place to live, but a renewed sense of human dignity. Being treated fairly and humanely buoys her with new boundaries and new hope.

The local police discover Tom's whereabouts, and he knows he must leave before they return with a warrant for his arrest. Even though he acted in self-defense, he knows from experience that civil judgment is often harsher for a poor man. Ma wants to hide Tom, but he will not let her. He has the beginnings of a social conscience and wants to find ways to correct the flaws in the social system. Ma is brokenhearted by Tom's departure, not really comprehending his talk about society's ills, but even her son's departure does not totally defeat her optimism. The family leaves the camp to get work in Fresno, and Pa Joad says, "You're the one that keeps us going, Ma." Ma explains that it is easier for a woman to adjust to changes as destiny deals out new cards, "A man lives . . . well, he sorta jerks. With a woman, it's all one flow, like a stream." Ma Joad's self-sacrificing optimism is seen, even by her, as some innate, biological predestination for all women, qualities that nature provides to a woman to help her cope. Some modern researchers have suggested that women live longer than men because women are more adaptable, that they survive because they fit themselves into a situation rather than altering the situation to fit their peculiarities. Ma Joad certainly lingers in film memory as a prominent figure not only for her survival techniques, but also for her successful application of those techniques in the face of all adversities.

The 1943 film production of Lillian Hellman's *Watch on the Rhine* presented an intimate look at a mother/daughter relationship that mirrored public sentiment concerning America's involvement in World War II. Sarah (Bette Davis) is the daughter of Fanny Farrelly (Lucille Watson, recreating her stage role and receiving an Academy Award nomination for Best Supporting Actress), a feisty, opinionated and ruling matriarch of a wealthy and well-connected political family in Washington. The time setting is 1941, just before the entry of the United States into the war. Fifteen years before, Sarah had married Kurt, a German patriot, and they had continued to live in Europe. When Hitler comes to power, Kurt becomes a leader of the anti-Nazi underground, and spends many years seeking to overthrow the Reich. As conditions worsen, he manages to get his wife and three children safely to the home of his mother-in-law, who has no knowledge of his political activities; to save an imprisoned friend who had once saved his life, however, Kurt must return to Germany.

Sarah's family is quite unable to grasp, at first, the ordeal Sarah and Kurt have endured for so many years, but Fanny welcomes them home enthusiastically, even offering to renovate an entire wing of her home for their personal use. Fanny is shocked to learn about her daughter's life over the years; in the beginning, Fanny possesses a naive sense of world problems and a false sense of security in believing that a mere ocean could isolate America from the horrors of Nazism. This unenlightened Fanny is representative of popular American beliefs about Europe, Fascism and the war in Europe prior to 1941—uncomprehending of the total picture, unaware of the terror to come, and confident that European troubles could not affect the American way of life.

When Sarah arrives at her mother's home, Fanny is already playing host to an exiled Romanian count and his American wife. The count is an opportunistic scoundrel, desperate for money; he tries to ingratiate himself with the Nazis at the German Embassy in hopes of improving his fortunes. Kurt's arrival offers a perfect occasion for blackmail, and he threatens to inform the Germans of Kurt's plan to release his friend from prison unless he is paid handsomely to remain silent. Kurt refuses to be blackmailed, but Fanny pays the Count's price. Distrusting that the Count will keep silent, Kurt kills him and leaves the country.

Sarah realizes she might not see Kurt again, but bravely watches him leave. The relationship between Sarah and Kurt has obviously been tested many times in the past, and their mutual love and respect allows each to understand what the other must do for a higher cause. After Kurt's departure, Fanny tells her daughter, "It's a fine thing to have you for a daughter, Sarah. I would like to have been like you." The audience comprehends, however, that Sarah is like Fanny, that Fanny is a strong woman who has just not realized the magnitude of the problem. Her somewhat startling epiphany, however, will keep her from future complacency. As Fanny comments to her son David, "Well, we've been shaken out of the magnolias." Indeed, Fanny and America realized their duty and found they had sufficient inner resources to meet the challenge. *Watch on the Rhine* was certainly a film of its time, elevating the war effort to a pedestal of nobility, and demonstrating that American motherhood could be there not only to roll bandages for the Red Cross but, most importantly, to allow their much-beloved sons to fight in the front lines.

The Wolf Man premiered in 1941, a "B" film tinkering with the age-old legends concerning werewolves, men who helplessly transform into monstrous predators at the sight of the full moon. Larry Talbot (Lon Chaney Jr.), younger son of a wealthy family, returns to his ancestral home in England after spending eighteen years in America.[27] As a lark, Talbot goes to a gypsy camp to have his fortune told. A pentagram, sign of the werewolf, is seen in the palm of his hand, marking him as the next victim. He survives the attack and kills the wolf, but is doomed to live as part man/part animal. The wise old gypsy woman, Maleva (Maria Ouspenskaya), was the mother of Bela, the werewolf killed by Talbot. She warns Talbot, in her quiet Russian accent, of the evil about to befall him, and gives him a necklace charm engraved with a pentagram to ward off the evil spell. Her own son had been the victim of the heinous affliction and she had been powerless to help, but she feels no hatred toward Talbot for killing her son—just pity and remorse for another young man's life going to waste. Instead of keeping the charm, Talbot gives it to a girl he likes, to protect her from him. He is a man possessed; he is mentally torn by his desire to be good and the overwhelming evidence that he is unable to control the evil aspect of his personality. The popularization of the psychological concepts of good versus evil are clearly visible in Talbot's tormented personality.

The old gypsy woman continues to help Larry as much as possible; when he, as werewolf, becomes ensnared in an animal trap, she is there to help release him. When, finally, Talbot is beaten with a silver-headed cane and returns to his human state in death, Maleva pronounces benediction over his still form, "As the rain enters the soil, the river enters the sea. So tears run to a predestined end. Your suffering is over. Now you will find peace for eternity." Maleva, small and wizened and reinforcing the maternal responsibilities of caring for her children, stood as the buffer between the "good" of Talbot and the "evil" of the werewolf. She showed compassion for children who were not evil by nature, but by circumstances and cruel turns of fate; in death, her children were restored to her sense of peace and cyclical righteousness.

Ethel Barrymore was an actress whose majestic presence imbued her motherly roles with dignity. In the 1944 RKO film, *None but the Lonely Heart*, Miss Barrymore played Ma Mott to Cary Grant's Ernie Mott. Both mother and son were rugged individualists, people who were capable of fighting their own battles. Their relationship was never dull, particularly because they were too much alike in temperament, and too quick to let pride and stubbornness guide their actions. Son Ernie is something of a wanderer, never staying in any one place for very long, and periodically returning home to Ma. Ma finally issues Ernie an ultimatum—stay put or stay away. Ma is terminally ill with cancer and desperately wants him to stay, but she is too proud to ask it of him directly. This inability of the mother and grown child to communicate easily with each other forms the basis of the dramatic tension in this movie. Ernie decides to leave and Ma tells him, "Someday you'll know I'm your only friend," a statement that proves prophetic.

Leaving town, Ernie is informed of his mother's medical condition by an old family friend. Suddenly, responsibility (which he had spent all his life trying to avoid) rears its intrusive head, and Ernie decides to stay in town and run the family's used furniture store. Ma is secretly pleased, but neither acts as if his decision is out of the ordinary, and both feign ignorance of Ma's condition.

Ma Mott worries about not leaving Ernie very much money when she dies, and so she violates her own honest standards by agreeing to sell items provided her by a shoplifting network; it is typical of a good mother that she acts wrongly only to help her child, not for self-serving purposes. Meanwhile Ernie, growing restless and frustrated, involves himself in a gang where money is easy to make and women are readily available.

Ma ultimately gets arrested for selling stolen goods, and ends up in the hospital, dying rapidly from the cancer. On her death-bed, she counsels Ernie, "Find a nice girl to look after you, a good girl. Something steady—nothing cheap, with a head on her shoulders. Forgive me, son. I disgraced ya." Ernie falls to her side, protesting it is not true, and begging her to live. At her death, Ernie senses he has lost everything important, that the world has finally defeated him. He had always complained that young people like himself had inherited a world that had been made impossible to live in by other people. At his mother's death, he realizes that he has to work to make things better, to face life offensively rather than defensively. He goes back to the girl who has loved him for years, a girl Ma had approved of, and seems to cope with his restlessness by recognizing the importance of belonging to a person, a place, and a time. Ma was, after all, Ernie's best friend.

Up to this point, little mention has been made concerning mothers who appeared in movie serials or "B" films who fit the category of inspirational mothers. Certainly, Fay Holden as the mother in the Andy Hardy series and Olive Blakeney as the mother in the Henry Aldrich stories, are two highly represent-ative examples of the type of mother found in so many Hollywood films in the thirties and early forties. Those two series, in particular, were tributes to the American ideal of the middle-class and small-town way of life. As David Zinman so effectively characterized the prevailing mood in these films, "In those halcyon days, houses had porches, cars had running boards and children walked to school. Kids thought 'pot' was what Mom cooked in. A 'joint' was a rundown establishment. And a 'dem-onstration' was when an auto salesman took you for a ride in a new model."[28] Those mothers were not particularly vital to the plot development, but their image of support and encourage-ment for their sons served to reinforce the state of normality the film producers were attempting to portray.

One serial mother who served as more than mere window-dressing for the American way of life, however, was first intro-duced as a character in *The Egg and I*, and went on to appear in several subsequent films about the antics of the rural Kettle family. Marjorie Main as Ma Kettle was a physically large woman, particularly in contrast to Pa (Percy Kilbride), her husband. *The Egg and I* is of interest not only for the characterization of Ma Kettle, but of several other older women as well.

Betty (Claudette Colbert) and Bob (Fred MacMurray) move from the city to a dilapidated chicken farm; he loves the idea—she is skeptical but dutifully follows him. The first people they meet are Mrs. Birdie Hicks (Esther Dale), a strong-minded older woman whose family is the most prominent in the county, and her mother, played by Isabel O'Madigan. The mother is quite old and portrayed as a genuine hypochondriac, always hoping for a new "condition" to treat. With all of her ailments, the mother is still livelier than Birdie, who functions in the film much like the character of Elvira Gulch in *The Wizard of Oz*. Birdie tries to control as much of the county as possible; her demeanor is stiff, humorless, and abruptly proper. Birdie is, without doubt, a woman of power; her characterization, however, shows how inappropriate and misplaced her power is outside the traditional setting of home. Ultimately, she is a woman who looks and acts like a man, a double sin for the era and one for which she is eventually punished.

Ma Kettle lives down the road from Betty and Bob, caring for innumerable children and her lazy, lackadaisical husband. Their house is ramshackle and disheveled—chickens have to be

shooed off the kitchen table so that supper can be served. Ma
tells Betty how she learned to live with the disorderliness, "I
said I can't make Pa change and be neat, so I'll have to change
and be dirty. Been peace in this house ever since." Ma accepts
as her duty the need to orient her style of living and approach
to homemaking to that of her husband, allowing him to set
the tone of the household, regardless of the seeming inappro-
priateness of the situation. Her respect for her husband as the
traditional "head of the house" marks Ma as a better wife than
a spotless house and impeccably groomed children ever could.
For the most part, the Kettles are caricatures of so-called hill-
billies, fulfilling the middle-class urban notion of what rural life
is all about. Ma Kettle, however, manages to transcend the
stereotype, masterfully holding together all the children and
the house in a decidedly better-humored manner than Birdie
Hicks could ever achieve. Ma's rules are few and her tolerance
level is high; she is the kind of mother few people have but
many wish for.

Betty grows more and more restless on the farm; it demands
too much effort for too few gratifications. One night when she
is alone, a little elderly woman, Emily (Ida Moore), appears on
the doorstep for a neighborly visit; she keeps talking to her
husband, Albert, who is invisible to all but her eyes. Emily tells
Betty about Charlotte, a six-foot chicken who drove her and
Albert off their chicken farm years before. The Sheriff shows
up to escort Emily back to the rest home she had wandered
away from; he tells Betty that Emily used to live on that very
farm with Albert until he ran away with another woman and
Emily went crazy because of it. Emily presents the one disturbing characterization in this otherwise comical film. She had
spent her entire life helping her husband in his work, but when
he left her he not only deserted her physically but also stole
her identity. She obviously had few coping mechanisms strong
enough to sustain her during such an emotional shock, and
retreated into a fantasy world where Albert still was a viable
part of her life. This is an all too real, and frightening, depiction
of what the culture's traditional sex role orientation can ultimately result in; a woman dependent on her husband for her
status in the community and her sense of personal identity
has very little left when he leaves or dies. Emily *does* frighten

Betty, who sees herself in a few years as another Emily. She packs her bags, unaware she is pregnant, and returns to the home of her wealthy but level-headed mother. Her mother (Elisabeth Risdon) encourages Betty to return to Bob, but Betty does not realize that is where she belongs until the baby is born. The sense of family—and the desire to protect and preserve that basic unit—sends Betty back to her husband.

Considered as a whole, *The Egg and I* is a funny, reassuring film, but the presence and implications of Emily show that, in 1947, new ideas and perceptions were beginning to make themselves known, though not necessarily for the better. With Ma Kettle, Birdie Hicks and Emily as role models, Betty has to choose the path Ma Kettle has paved; mean Birdie and crazy Emily, both childless, were too vivid possibilities of life outside the expected route of motherhood for American women.

To summarize the category of "Mother Faithful" is to point to several recurring attributes of the women who fit into this particular category. They are strong, devoted mothers whose sense of self-sacrifice occasionally crosses the thin boundary into masochism. They are revered by their families, and recognized as special people. They are not perceived only as people who give of themselves to their children, however, for their children are portrayed as insurance against insanity and insecurity for a faithful mother in her old age. They are very often widows—even at relatively young ages—who must draw deeply on their powers of persistence and fortitude to be both mother and father to their children. They are the mothers that children would choose as their very own, if such a choice were possible. They are the mothers that songs are written about. They are, indeed, the women Mother's Day was established to honor.

There is a fine line of distinction between good mothers of the first and second aspect; if not for cruel or unjust twists of fate which she could not control, almost any mother within the second aspect of "Mother Faithful" might well have taken her proper position in the fullest sense of the definition.

Mothers in this second aspect are very close in spirit to "Mother Faithful"; the difference is in the children they reared. Unfortunate though it may be, mothers are often judged in terms of how well their children mature into adulthood. This standard allows mothers to be endlessly praised for successful children (indeed, they are the source of her success), and forever pitied for erring or evil offspring (the source of her lasting shame and sorrow).

These mothers are good women who raised their children with proper values and social standards, but who all "failed" in the opinion of the world because their children failed. In each case, the child learns with the greatest difficulty that Mom was right after all.

In 1930, the first talking gangster film premiered,[29] *Little Caesar*, starring Edward G. Robinson. It began a trend of successful crime movies that would continue through the thirties. Our concern does not focus on Rico, the swaggering protagonist (though his lack of family ties could be interpreted as part of the reason for his misdirected energies into crime rather than respectable living), but rather a minor member of Rico's gang, Tony, who drives Rico's car. Tony is a young man from a poor family, attracted to the glamour of easy money and little work promised by the gang. Eventually, his Italian immigrant mother is able to help him see that he is not living a good, nor ultimately fruitful, life. Talking to Tony, she says, "You used to be a good boy, Antonio. Remember when you used to sing in the choir?" Tony, remorseful, is reconciled to her and decides to leave the gang; Rico, however, strongly believes that loyalty to the gang supersedes loyalty to family or God. As Tony is going to meet the parish priest to confess his crimes, Rico shoots and kills him on the steps of the church. Tony is buried in grand gangland style, with Rico the chief mourner at the funeral—his death had been a business matter, nothing personal. The only consolation Tony's mother has is that her son had renounced his life of crime and had intended to live according to the values she had worked to instill in him in his childhood.

From a nonfiction and best selling book, *I Am a Fugitive From a Chain Gang* came to the screen in 1932. It qualifies as one of the most bleak and depressing films of the thirties era, a genuine attempt at social commentary. It is the story of a World War I veteran, James Allen (Paul Muni) who returns from Europe with great hopes of becoming an engineer but faces, instead, the stark reality of returning to his old job as an inventory clerk in a factory. Desperate and frustrated, he leaves home

in search of construction work. His life turns into a series of
misunderstandings and misfortunes, caused by forces he neither
sees nor has the ability to counteract. He is a social innocent
who becomes a social outcast. His mother is quiet and retiring;
when James first returns from the war, she and her minister
son encourage James to resume his old job, to choose the
security of the familiar position and accept the boredom it
holds out to him. When James decides to look for other work,
however, his mother is supportive; she tells him she knows he
must do what he thinks is right, and gives her approval to his
aspirations.

The irony in this film is that James Allen *is* a good man,
faithful to the values he was raised by; he is, however, a victim of
a bureaucracy that cares little for the rights of individuals, and a
society that insists on telling him that his values are worthless. The
message of the film is devastating because it says that the old
standards cannot support the new structure, and James Allen
is left a psychological, emotional and physical fugitive—a man
who cannot find a place where he belongs because he has no
coping mechanisms left to him. It does not matter what his
widowed mother taught him as a child because her teachings
no longer apply; one cannot teach norms in a norm-less society.
As Bergman commented so incisively on the overall impact of
this film, "The national landscape seemed like an empty lot."[30]
It was a world where even the social power of motherhood had
no meaning.

Back Street (1932) starred Irene Dunne as Ray Schmidt, a
reckless young woman who becomes involved in a lifelong
affair with a successful banker, and Jane Darwell as Jane Schmidt,
Ray's conservative and disapproving mother. Ray lives in Cin-
cinnati, a town she finds insufferably staid and boring; she
dances every night away and longs for excitement in her life.
Mrs. Schmidt, not sure why Ray cannot be content in the city
where she was raised, comments, "Girls of today have no joy
in the simple pleasures of home. This younger generation is
going to the dogs." Her comment proves ironic, for Ray discovers eventually that she values the very things her mother
values, home and family.

Ray falls in love with a married man, Walter, and allows

him to support her for twenty-five years (though he certainly
is not overly generous in that regard). She gives up her promising business career, forgoes children of her own, and waits
day after day for the few hours her married lover can spare
her. Ray grows old with mounting frustrations about her lack
of personal fulfillment, but remains unable to break the emotional bond between herself and the banker. When her lover suffers
a stroke and dies, the little significance life held for Ray dies
also; for no explainable medical reason, Ray rests her head near
a picture of Walter, says, "I'm coming, Walter, I'm coming"
and dies. The melodramatic ending makes a peculiar kind of
sense—Walter was Ray's life, the very reason she existed, and
the end of his life meant the end of hers as well. Her mother
had been correct: the simple pleasures of home—husband and
children—were the elements of lifelong happiness. Her refusal
to heed maternal advice provokes an appropriate punishment,
the denial of the assumed joys of maternity to Ray, and a subsequent life devoid of significant achievement or personal
satisfaction.

Most immigrant mothers encountered in the films of the
thirties were of European origin. One interesting exception
occurred in the film *Bordertown*, a 1934 vehicle for Paul Muni
(as Johnny Ramirez) and Bette Davis (as Marie Roark), with
Soledad Jimenez as Johnny's mother. Johnny had been a tough
kid, growing up in the barrio in Los Angeles. With the encouragement of his mother, he manages to complete night law
school, with lofty ambitions of helping people with their
troubles. His devoted widowed mother sells her wedding ring
to pay for a nameplate for Johnny's graduation gift; she had
always believed in his goodness and his native abilities, and he
rewards her faith with deep love and promises to buy her everything she wants when he meets with financial success.

Unfortunately, Johnny's law practice does not do well; he
has many clients, but their problems are small and his fees
nonexistent. Johnny finally gets a case worth his effort; a rich
young woman drunkenly runs her car into an old man's vegetable
truck. Armed with righteous indignation and his mother's
prayer—"Please, Holy Mother, make it for my Juanito to win
his case. Many times I ask you to help him, but this time it

would break his heart. Help him, Blessed Mary. I don't want the
fur coat, I only want him to win"—Johnny engages the rich,
establishment lawyer hired by the woman's family to defend
her. Though his client is in the right, Johnny's inadequacies as
a lawyer cause the case to be thrown out of court. Disillusioned
and cynical, he decides that money is the key to power and
to getting along in the white man's world, and that he must
leave home to pursue those key elements. His old mother cannot understand why he wants to leave:

MAMACITA: Here is your home. Here is all the people who
    know you and love you.

JOHNNY: The people who love me are poor—dirt—like I am.
    They can't give me what I need, and I won't be dirt anymore.

The remainder of the movie chronicles Johnny's journey,
physically and emotionally, to the discovery that his people
do matter to him, and that it is vital to remember who you are
and where you come from.
    Johnny goes on the road, and after a year finds steady em-
ployment as a floor manager and bouncer in a rundown casino
in Bordertown. He proves himself a genuine asset to the business
and convinces the owner, Charlie, to sell him part of the business. Charlie's young wife, Marie, makes constant amorous
advances toward Johnny, which he consistently ignores. Marie,
in hopes of capturing Johnny's attention, kills Charlie one
night by leaving him, quite drunk, in the garage with the car
engine running. Johnny, assuming Charlie to be a suicide victim,
becomes manager of the casino, turning it into an elegant re-
treat for rich patrons from north of the border. He falls in love
with one of his chic customers and Marie, angered by his inat-
tention to her, tells Johnny that she murdered Charlie so that
they could be together. Outraged at her cold-bloodedness,
Johnny orders Marie to stay away from him and from the casino.
To gain revenge, Marie goes to the police and claims Johnny forced
her to kill Charlie and he is arrested for complicity. Johnny's
mother visits him in prison while he awaits trial, still believing
in him; to the priest she affirms, "Sometimes he bad, but never

my Juanito lie." His statement of innocence is enough reassur-
ance for his mother. The criminal charges against Johnny are
dropped when Marie is certified insane. Trying to reestablish
his life, Johnny asks the woman customer to marry him, but
she refuses because he is not her social equal. He sells the casino,
uses the money to endow his old law school, and goes back to
the barrio "with my own people," his beaming mother at his
side. Johnny, who had turned his back on the simple and un-
assuming ways of his mother, realized through his own experiences that money and power were not the elements that identified a man, but rather that who he was and what he believed
in were the forces that shaped his destiny.

With modern eyes, we might deplore the seemingly inherent
lesson regarding ethnicity and social class, that a man wishing
to better himself was defeated by outside barriers of racism
and class consciousness. Contemporary movie reviews, however,
did not dwell on these concerns and it remains unproven that
this would have been an issue recognized by the audience in
1934. *Bordertown* is another example of the oft-repeated lesson
in the thirties that people should be content with what they
already have, that lust for money or power or excitement will
only lead to disappointment, and that mothers have a magical
ability to recognize this as a fact of life.

Bette Davis, quite possibly the most versatile dramatic actress
in American film, was awarded her second Academy Award for
Jezebel, her 1938 version of the spoiled, high spirited Southern
belle whose selfish actions lead to unhappiness for many people.
Set in New Orleans in 1852, Fay Bainter portrayed Aunt Belle
to Davis's Julie (a role which won Bainter an Academy Award
as Best Supporting Actress). Aunt Belle raised Julie, but Julie's
actions are in stark contrast to the refined gentility Belle attempted to instill in her. Julie insists on outraging society by
flouting local customs at every opportunity, a practice which
eventually causes her fiance, Preston Dillard (Henry Fonda),
to break their engagement. Preston leaves town for a year;
Julie realizes her mistakes and anxiously awaits his return. When
Preston does come home to help during an epidemic, he brings
his Northern bride, Amy, with him. Julie does her best to compromise the marriage, finally encouraging her current suitor to

fight a duel for her honor. Aunt Belle warns Julie, "We women can start the men quarreling often enough; we can't ever stop them," but Julie pushes on in her pursuit of Preston. When the duel ends in her suitor's death and Julie shows no remorse, Aunt Belle has far harsher words for Julie, "I'm thinking of a woman called Jezebel, who did evil in the sight of God." Jezebel, the wife of Ahab, king of Israel, was a shameless, abandoned woman who was notorious for her behavior; her story is recorded in the Book of Kings in the Old Testament. Very often, older women in films during this period acted as repositories of cultural mores, warning transgressors of the doom their actions would precipitate; Aunt Belle is a perfect example of this type of modern doom-sayer.

Julie discovers that Preston has become ill with yellow fever. She manages to go to him and nurse him, but city officials insist he be sent to the island for fever victims, a veritable death yard from which few returned. Julie begs Amy to allow her to accompany Preston to the island, to prove she can be strong and generous and noble; Amy allows Julie to go, realizing that Julie is sincere in her need to cleanse herself by an unselfish act. The final scene of the movie stands perhaps as one of the most melodramatically staged scenes in all of American film. Julie is seated on an open wagon, with feverish Preston's head in her lap and surrounded by other fever victims, riding through the human misery that was New Orleans during the time of the epidemic. The wagon passes a huge bonfire in the street—thought to control the spread of disease—with Julie, looking like a classic Madonna, silhouetted against the leaping flames, so symbolic as the cleansing agent of her soul. For the first time in her life, Julie realizes the importance of selflessness, though it may cost her her health and possibly her life. Aunt Belle's shining example of hospitality and generosity throughout the film came to fruition at last in the child she had raised. The message is clear—a woman is at her best when devoting herself to the needs of others.

Sergeant York (1941) starred Gary Cooper in the title role and Margaret Wycherly as his enduring mountain mother. It is a story, unlike others within this aspect, that ends happily. Set in the backwoods of Tennessee in 1916, it focuses on the

York family, poor sharecroppers who have no material wealth
to speak of but a full measure of family love and solidarity.
Alvin (Cooper) is the oldest of Widow York's three children;
he is a hard working but undisciplined young man, who seeks
relief from his daily drudgery by drinking moonshine and ca-
rousing with his friends for entertainment. Mother York, a
quiet and religious woman, does not condemn Alvin's actions—
recognizing the impossible work he must do to "get corn out
of rocks"—but she feels a "little religion wouldn't hurt" Alvin,
and prays for his enlightenment.

Alvin falls in love with a beautiful young woman, Gracie
Williams (Joan Leslie) and is determined to win her affections
by working hard enough to be able to afford a piece of rich
bottom land. He toils for many months at any odd job he can
find, but ultimately falls short of the purchase price by a few
dollars and loses his option on the land. Mother York encourages
Alvin, but she warns him that his father had attempted the
same thing and failed; regardless, she approves of Alvin's determination, thankful he is finally channeling his energies in more
positive directions. The failure to get the land sends Alvin into
a tirade; he gets drunk and decides to ride off on his horse in
the middle of a violent electrical storm to beat the man who
double-crossed him. Riding along, he is struck by lightning and
subsequently stunned into a religious commitment by the
experience. His mother is overjoyed at his change of heart, and
watches proudly as Alvin works to become an upstanding citizen
in the community.

World War I finds Alvin drafted into the army, even though
he registered as a conscientious objector. He is a model soldier,
but harbors great reservations about killing. He finally comes
to a realization that he, as a citizen of a democracy, has a vested
interest in the war; he realizes that he is fighting to preserve his
right to live in Tennessee, his right to try to own bottom land,
and his right to marry Gracie and raise a family in peace. At
this point in the film, the inspirational message intended for the
1941 audience is made abundantly clear—Americans fight only
to defend their rights, not to oppress other nations or steal
the possessions of others. War is a sacred, though unpleasant,
necessity forced on Americans by the greed of others.

Alvin, shipped to France, emerges from the war with the Congressional Medal of Honor and a hero's welcome in the United States. In his suite of rooms at the Waldorf Astoria, a picture of his frail-looking mother awaits him (a gesture that he dearly appreciated), and the first person he talks to on the telephone is Mother York. When Alvin finally gets home to Tennessee, he steps off the train to a tumultuous greeting, but looks confused and searching until he spies his old mother at the end of the crowd, standing and waiting patiently for him. Their greeting is simple, as are they, but touching:

ALVIN: I'm home, Ma.

MOTHER: I'm glad, son.

Alvin's basic sense of goodness and righteousness obviously came from what he had been taught by his mother; his fierce sense of independence and need to work hard also came from Mother York. Her humility and pride were evident in the simple but straightforward blessing she always pronounced before eating, "The Lord bless these victuals we got and help us to beholden to no one. Amen." This style of independence and self-sufficiency were the types of attributes Americans in 1941 wanted to believe were the elements that set them off from the rest of the world. As wartime propaganda (though this term is not being used pejoratively), Alvin and his mother were very effective role models. Mother York begins the film belonging to the category of "Mother Long-suffering" but ends it very conclusively in the category of "Mother Faithful."

To summarize the manifestation of the good mother who suffers because of her children, is to realize, initially, that a woman in this role is not there because of her actions or inadequacies as a mother. She is placed in her unenviable position by the actions of her children, who are usually influenced adversely by forces outside the home, forces that the mother cannot understand or control. Mothers in this category usually live to see their children realize their mistakes, but it is often too late for the children to be restored to their mothers. The mothers of this category are the mothers country songs are

written about, but the songs are generally sad ballads rather
than raucous songs of celebration.

The third manifestation of good mothers, "Mother Absent",
is more difficult to deal with, and encountered far less frequently, because it is comprised of mothers who never appear
on screen yet are significant to their children because of their
very absence. These are mothers who are removed from a child's
life by death or other unavoidable circumstances. These are
mothers whom we know little about—whether good, bad or
indifferent as maternal figures—but mothers who have left a
legacy in the emotional and psychological scars borne by their
children throughout their lives. This aspect, then, is much more
concerned with the child than the mother herself. Though the
category is slight in terms of examples, it is a distinct group
that warrants exploration.

Each Dawn I Die (1939), contains both a "Mother Faithful"
and a "Mother Absent." It is the story of two men, Frank Ross
(James Cagney) and "Hood" Stacey (George Raft). Both Ross
and Stacey grew up in impoverished areas of the city, both
despise crooked police and politicians, but each goes in a separate direction as an adult to attempt to remedy the corrupt
situations that they encounter. Ross chooses to be a news-
paperman who can expose lawlessness; Stacey, cynical about
justice, chooses a life as a criminal. The biggest situational
difference between the two is that Ross has a living mother and
Stacey does not.

Frank Ross is involved in writing stories exposing the illegal
activities of the local district attorney; for his efforts, he is
framed on a manslaughter charge and goes to prison. His elderly
mother writes and visits frequently, even though the sight of
her son in prison overwhelms her emotionally after she leaves;
in front of Frank, she is stoic, cheerful and concerned only
with keeping his spirits and hopes elevated.

Stacey, though a criminal, has a well developed sense of ethics
and justice. Incarcerated in the same facility with Ross, he
manages to break out and work to vindicate his friend because
he believes in Ross' innocence. Stacy discovers that the hoodlum who framed Ross is also in the same prison, so Stacey gives
himself up to the police to get back into the jail. During an

attempted prison break by other inmates, Stacey is fatally
wounded but manages to force the framer to confess in front
of the warden and Ross is cleared. The warden is perplexed
about why Stacey was so involved in attempting to help Ross;
Stacey explains that while he has wasted his own life, Ross
would go on to live the kind of life he might have led if he had
had the right kind of "breaks" as a child, with a loving family
life and a devoted mother. Even though his mother is not present, Stacey reveres motherhood and what a good mother means
to a child's development; he is willing to risk his own life, so
that Ross can leave prison and resume a noble, virtuous existence. Stacey's brand of honor among thieves establishes him
as a noble man as well, who unfortunately chose the socially
unacceptable path of lawlessness; he did not so much disdain
the law, but rather the hypocrites elected to enforce it. Stacey's
self-sacrifice is a bit naive in terms of the story line, but George
Raft manages to make it believable and sympathetic.

A second gangster film that serves as an example of this
aspect of absent mothers is *High Sierra* (1941), starring Humphrey Bogart as bank robber Roy Earle. Earle escapes from
jail in Illinois and travels west toward the Nevada-California
border, to the High Sierras, to plan a robbery in Los Angeles.
On the road, Earle meets the Goodhue family, an elderly couple
(Henry Travers and Elisabeth Risdon) and their pretty teenaged
granddaughter on their way to Los Angeles. The first meeting
is brief, but they are destined to serve an important function
in Earle's life, as foils who allow the audience to see his gentle
personality traits in action.

Earle comes upon the Goodhues again at the scene of a minor
car accident in which they are involved. He helps them talk
their way out of any blame, and even convinces the other driver
to pay the Goodhues one hundred dollars in damages. Earle
then takes the family to an auto park. Pa Goodhue is fond of
talking and philosophizing; Ma is quiet but obviously humored
by Pa's endless monologue. They are good, solid people from
Ohio who lost their farm and are heading for a new start in
California. The young granddaughter, Velma, is crippled with
a club foot; Earle offers to finance the necessary medical treatment once they are settled in Los Angeles. When Earle is with

the Goodhues, he is kind and considerate; his "tough guy"
facade disappears and he is genuinely protective of these simple,
loving people. Ma Goodhue always greets Roy affectionately,
as if he were her own son; indeed, she takes the place of the
mother Earle never knew. Earle's relationship with the Goodhues, particularly his tender affection for Ma, strongly establishes his anti-hero status; he is a tough, no nonsense criminal,
but he also possesses a remarkably strong sense of righteousness and propriety when confronted by people who are
down on their luck through no fault of their own. This motif
of innocent people buffeted by the seemingly uncontrolla-
ble and cruel movements of fate is a direct response to the
stunning capriciousness of the Depression, which ultimately
affected people of all economic levels and shook the very foun-
dations of the national belief in individualism and the work
ethic. People who wanted to work, and to whom work equaled
personal worth, found themselves unable to do so. The national
economic collapse pointed out only too well how interconnected
and interdependent the diverse elements of the American society
had become. The audience viewing *High Sierra* is led to the
conclusion that no man can be all bad if he treats an old woman
like Ma Goodhue with love and deference.

Roy and his accomplices rob a large hotel of jewelry and
cash. One of the getaway cars explodes in a fiery crash, and
the law officials are quickly on Roy's trail. Before he leaves
Los Angeles, however, he stops at the Goodhues to see Velma
walk after her surgery. Leaving quickly, he is chased up Mount
Whitney, where he is trapped by the police but manages to hold
them at arm's length for several hours with a machine gun.
Earle is determined not to go back to prison; he refuses to
surrender and the police eventually kill him. Earle is dead,
but his dignity is intact and the sympathies of the audience
rest, as with so many gangster films, on the wrong side of the law.
Because Earle is presented as a total personality—neither all
bad nor all good—his death is, in a strange way, the death of
a hero. Bosley Crowther said it best in a review which appeared
in the *New York Times* in 1941: "He dies gallantly. It's a wonder
the American flag wasn't wrapped about his broken corpse."[31]

The film which best illustrates the category of "Mother

Absent" is probably also the most over-analyzed popular film
in American history, *Citizen Kane* (1941). The opening shots of
Xanadu, Kane's vast mansion, show decay and gloom; this was
not meant to be a happy story, nor a story of success, but
rather a chronicle of one man's ultimate failure. The story of
Charles Foster Kane (Orson Welles) is told in flashback, as a
reporter attempts to discover the meaning of Kane's dying word,
"Rosebud."

Kane's mother (Agnes Moorehead) owns a boarding house
in Colorado; as payment for back rent, a destitute miner gives
her the deed to a mine, which turns out to be a gold mine. She
takes the vast fortune provided by the mine and places it in a
trust fund in Charles' name. She sends young Charles, only
eight years of age, to the East; he is placed under the guardian-
ship of a conservative banker, to be educated and raised as
would befit a man who would one day inherit the sixth largest
personal fortune in the world. Charles is confused about why
he has been sent away from his home in Colorado (indeed, his
father opposes the action but is too weak to overrule his wife),
and he spends the rest of his life searching for love—in his public and private lives—though it always eludes him. Kane is a
collector—of art, of people—but he never gathers enough material
possessions to compensate for what he left behind in Colorado
so many years before. His emotional life never matures very far
beyond that of an eight year old boy; his life is overshadowed
by the "loss" of his mother, who sends him away at such an
early age. Indeed, his dying thought is of the simple, wooden
sled he was riding the day he was sent away from his childhood
home, the sled which had the word "Rosebud" emblazoned
on its top side.

Kane is an intelligent man who is perpetually hampered by
his emotional immaturity. Even he acknowledges the degree to
which he is spoiled when he tells a friend, "You know, Mr.
Bernstein, if I hadn't been very rich, I might have been a really
great man." The vast amounts of money he controls cannot buy
the one thing he needs most desperately, a loving mother and
a secure home. Mrs. Kane, who never appears in the film after
the early Colorado episode, nevertheless manages to dominate
the outcome of her son's life.

The summary of this third manifestation, though short on
examples, is quite long in significance. It is this category that
so thoroughly carries the message of what the lack of a faithful
mother can mean to a child's development. These are the mothers for whom our own reactions are so ambiguous, for whom
a strong love/hate relationship exists—they are loved and needed
because they are mothers, yet hated for their inability (even
if they are not to blame for their absence) to fulfill their maternal role. It is neither an enviable position for the mothers
nor their children. These are the mothers who make the women
in the "Mother Faithful" category look better than ever.

The film mothers who constitute the more negative maternal
examples—the scatterbrained mothers—seem indigenous to the
Depression era of the thirties. In a time frame during which the
average middle-class person in the film audience could appreciate
the financial difficulties facing the country, the rich provided
a common ground for satirization and parody; the audience
could view the absurdity of the petty problems of the wealthy
characters without being personally threatened. Just as many
horror films were set in Europe to keep personal association
away from the American audience, so too did the wealthy
provide a "foreign" setting for the majority of the movie patrons.
Interestingly enough, few wealthy old men were encountered
in the films researched, but rich elderly women abounded. Why
might this discrepancy exist in the different portrayals of men
and women who had a common characterization of wealth?
Rich men were often portrayed as self-made men, Horatio Alger
stories come to life, who spoiled their wives and children by
providing an endless procession of material goods. Rich women,
however, seemed to suffer from cultural stereotypes that held as
fact that women had no conception of the value of money
except in terms of how many china place settings or other
needless luxuries it could purchase.

Rich mothers of this category appear foolish and silly because of their money and their lack of needing to work for a
living or worry about where the rent money would be found;
the lack of needing to suffer or wanting to nurture seems to
remove their maternal credibility. Rich women could be safely
ridiculed because their existence was self-centered and parasitic,

blatantly displaying their collective disassociation from work and responsibility. Ironically, these characteristics combine to form the ultimate expression of the real effects of pedestal sitting—bored women who consider their lack of structured responsibility to be a sign of social achievement and whose attentions turn inward, for lack of a better focus, to petty and silly concerns.

Rich men do not generally receive the same heavy-handed treatment, primarily because a rich man has a successful company or high-ranking position as "proof" of, and reward for, his hard work. Rich women, traditionally associated with households peopled by assorted maids and butlers who perform her traditional tasks, have no such compelling evidence of anything other than a unique ability to choose potential millionaires for husbands. The parasitic nature of these wealthy dowagers makes them fair game for the derision and scorn of a Depression audience. The lesson to the audience is plain—wealth does not automatically produce happiness or contentment. Money may not be the root of all evil, but it certainly seems to be held accountable for an intense degree of human foolishness and nonsensical behavior.

Perhaps the classic example of a scatterbrained[32] mother appeared in *My Man Godfrey* (1936) in the character of Angelica Bullock (Alice Brady), one of the most ridiculous rich women to ever appear in films. This was a movie which incorporated social conditions of the Depression into a comedic format with a high level of success; in other words, the film delivered homely truths without depressing the audience emotionally.

As the film opens, the Bullocks are involved in a charity scavenger hunt, collecting such unlikely items as goats, corsets, monkeys and a "Forgotten Man" (a euphemism for one of the countless unemployed men who populated the shanty towns hastily erected near large cities). Sisters Cornelia (Gail Patrick) and Irene (Carole Lombard) both discover Godfrey (William Powell) and each attempts to pay him to appear as their "prize." Cornelia is snobbish and rude; Godfrey pushes her into an ash pile. Irene, however, is a different sort—spoiled and precocious, but not vicious; Godfrey agrees to accompany her, "to beat Cornelia." At the hotel where the hunt results are being tabu-

lated, Godfrey exhibits more innate refinement and grace than
any of the guests; his assessment of the "hunters" as "empty-
headed nitwits" convinces Irene that she wants Godfrey as her
protege and she hires him as the family butler.

The Bullock household contains somewhat less discipline
than the city zoo; Cornelia drives a car through a store window
and Irene rides a horse home in the middle of the night, leaving
it to graze in her father's library. Mrs. Bullock drinks too much
and sees "pixies" the morning after; she allows a free-loader,
a so-called protege, to live in the house and help himself to
her husband's money in the name of art. Her vocal pattern is
an uninterrupted line of near-hysterical outbursts. Her sensitivity to other people borders on the ludicrous; when Cornelia
criticizes Irene's hiring of Godfrey, Mrs. Bullock replies, "Godfrey is the first thing Irene has shown affection for since her
Pomeranian died last month," as if a human being could serve
as an amusement or project for a "Park Avenue brat" (as Godfrey so refreshingly characterizes the daughters).

Mr. Bullock, played by gravel-voiced Eugene Pallette, is the
one seemingly sane member of the family. When he attempts
to tell the family that they are overspending and will have to
economize, the girls become bored and his wife chides him
"not to start that again." Mr. Bullock insists the family needs
discipline, but he never really forces any reduction in their
extravagant living standards. Financial matters worsen, and Mr.
Bullock's company is rescued by Godfrey, who turns out to
be a member of a wealthy Boston family; he dresses as a bum
and works as a butler in an attempt to discover what poor people
really need. Godfrey finds good in all people; as he says, "The
only difference between a derelict and a man is a job." After
his true identity is revealed, he goes about helping the men he
had lived with at the landfill site, providing jobs and dignity for
those whom society had cast aside. In an ending that could
only have occurred in a genuine screwball comedy, spoiled
Irene convinces noble Godfrey that they should be married,
though any attraction between the two had previously been
generated only by Irene.

While Godfrey emerges as a character worth emulating, the
rest of the Bullocks seem hardly touched by his example. Mrs.

Bullock, in particular, worries when bankruptcy looms as a strong possibility; avoiding such a fate, however, seems to generate no new behavior on her part. She remains as fiscally irresponsible as before; the audience is left with no real sense of remorse on her part or promises for better behavior. She seems incapable of changing her ways, and the audience is left to surmise that once a featherbrain, always a featherbrain.

Another film featuring Alice Brady somewhat reversed the situation of *My Man Godfrey*, but resulted in much the same outcome. *Gold Diggers of 1935*, perhaps best remembered for its Busby Berkeley number involving row after row of choreographed white baby grand pianos, finds Brady as Mrs. Matilda Prentiss, the rich but miserly widow of a man who made his fortune manufacturing flypaper. The sticky and entrapping qualities of flypaper are all too symbolic of Mrs. Prentiss' attitude toward money—get it and keep it. The film opens at the Wentworth Hotel, an exclusive resort playground for the wealthy, where Mrs. Prentiss has arrived for the season with playboy son Humbolt and shy daughter Ann in tow. Dick Powell plays Dick Curtis, a medical student working as the head hotel clerk during the summer.

Much of the humor of the film revolves around Mrs. Prentiss' frugality. She gives four bellboys a total of twenty-five cents for carrying sixteen suitcases; when her son objects, she replies, "Just because I happen to be rich, I have no intention of being imposed upon." Mrs. Prentiss dominates everyone and everything around her; she is determined to see Ann married to a very eccentric and unexciting millionaire, whose passionate interest in life is researching and publishing the definitive history of snuff boxes. Even when Mrs. Prentiss sponsors the annual charity show at the hotel, she cautions the stage director, "Remember, everything is to be small and cheap." The audience sees Mrs. Prentiss faint at losing money in the stock market and be "reduced" to having only thirty million dollars left to her name; she can only be perceived as silly and ridiculous—no woman with that much money could gather much sympathy from a Depression era audience. Matilda is so involved in holding on to every single cent of her money that she forgets to enjoy herself, and again the message is clear—money does not necessarily buy

happiness and can, in fact, breed greater discontent and unhappiness.

So standard was Alice Brady's portrayal of wealthy women
that she appeared in another similar role in the 1936 Irene Dunne
vehicle, *Joy of Living*. Dunne portrays Maggie Garret, the "first
lady" of Broadway who earns ten thousand dollars a week and
supports a leeching family—including mother Minerva (played
by Brady), father, sister, brother-in-law, and twin nieces—who
manage to spend every cent she brings home. Maggie never
really enjoys herself, always worrying about how to make enough
money to keep her family happy. Rather than being appreciative
of Maggie's generosity, the family is overbearing in attitude and
always demanding more from her. A knight in shining armor
appears in the character of Daniel Brewster (Douglas Fairbanks,
Jr.), who wants Maggie to sail away with him to the South
Pacific, leaving the free-loading family behind to fend for themselves. Brewster, himself, belongs to a rich and high-powered
family of bankers but has broken away from them to live a
slow-paced life in perpetually beautiful weather on an island
he happens to own.

Through a complicated set of developments, Maggie marries
Dan on the spur of the moment but assumes they will remain
in New York City because of her career and her family. Confused at his refusal to agree to that scenario, she leaves him. Her
family greets her with venomous denunciations upon her return,
with Minerva leading the group, chastising Maggie for being so
selfish and self-centered as to run off with Dan. Maggie finally
realizes that the family does not really care about her but about
her paycheck; she tells them good-bye and rushes to the dock just
in time to join Dan and sail away. Minerva is a bad mother;
allowing her daughter to support her, she becomes more and
more demanding instead of appreciating the generosity her
daughter displays toward her. With the various duties of mothers
that have been outlined within this chapter, it is obvious that
Minerva cannot be allowed to continue exploiting her own child.
Again, within the comedic form, Minerva is made to appear
frivolous and empty-headed, unworthy of any devotion from
her children. Portrayed unsympathetically, she is not a character
that the audience worries about as Maggie sails away with her
husband to a life uncluttered by free-loaders and ingrates.

There Goes the Groom, a comedy released in 1937, had its
most humorous moments in the performance of Mary Boland
as Mrs. Genevieve Russell, grand matriarch of her family of
formerly rich people trying to cope with a cash flow problem
of gigantic proportions. The rich, being accustomed to excess
money, seldom consider going to work as a means of relieving
financial difficulties; indeed, Mrs. Russell's scheme to regain
financial solvency rests on her ability to recruit a wealthy son-
in-law for one of her two daughters, Janet or Betty (Ann Sothern). Mrs. Russell is flighty, opportunistic and obnoxious, the
exact qualities needed to implement her plan.

Dick Matthews (Burgess Meredith), away in Alaska for
three years working his gold mine, returns to San Francisco to
the girl he hopes is still waiting for him, Janet Russell. Janet,
however, is engaged to someone else; her younger sister, Betty,
is in love with Dick but he is not in the mood to notice. Dick,
as a friendly gesture, takes Betty to his yacht; Mrs. Russell
misinterprets his actions, and is outraged. To cover up, Dick
proposes to Betty. Suddenly, "Mama" Russell is thrilled, calling
Dick "Dickie Wickie" and "Duckie Wuckie," seeing him—and
his gold mine—as the answer to all the family's money problems.
Betty is the only member of the family who truly wants Dick,
not his money. Janet breaks her engagement; Dick, still in love
with her, wants to break his engagement to Betty, but hesitates
to hurt her. Mrs. Russell plans an elaborate wedding, the rehearsal for which is a total fiasco. The rehearsal convinces Dick
that he does not want to marry into the crazy family, so he
feigns amnesia to absolve himself of his promise. So intent is
Mrs. Russell on spending Dick's money, however, that she
exclaims, "A man doesn't have to be in his right mind to get
married, does he?" Her motives are clearly selfish, and the
opportunity is prime for someone to put her in her place. Betty
tells her mother what she thinks of her attempted manipulation
of Dick; Dick, seeing that Betty loves him for himself, marries
her. Mrs. Russell acquires her rich son-in-law, but under far
different conditions than she ever imagined. As in the previous
movies discussed, the motives and actions of the elderly rich
mother character are not intended for emulation, but as further
evidence that money—or the quest for it—serves as a corrupting
influence for the majority of people involved.

Frank Capra's film, *You Can't Take It With You* (1938), presents the conflict between big, rich companies and small, powerless individuals, the former trying to bulldoze the latter in order to make greater profits. Anthony P. Kirby owns a banking monopoly that plans to make a fortune on the coming war; he wants to buy twelve city blocks surrounding a munitions factory so that when the factory wishes to expand, it will have to deal exclusively with him. All the local residents sell their homes to Kirby except Martin Vanderhof (Lionel Barrymore), whose home is a refuge for eccentrics—people who could only be described as free spirits. Vanderhof's daughter, Penny Syca-more (Spring Byington) lives with him, as does her husband, her daughter Alice (Jean Arthur), and a host of unrelated, idiosyncratic people. Tony Kirby (James Stewart) is vice-president of his father's firm, but his heart is not really in his work; Alice Sycamore is his secretary, with whom he is in love.

Mrs. Anthony P. Kirby (Mary Forbes) is rich and proper and socially conscious; she is distressed by Tony's affection for Alice. Determined to marry Alice, Tony arranges for his parents to have dinner at the Vanderhof's, a scene that can only be compared to Amy Vanderbilt dining at an amusement park; complete chaos reigns. The evening progresses steadily downhill, culminating with all the fireworks stored in the basement going off accidentally and everyone in the house, including the Kirbys, being arrested for disturbing the peace.

In night court, Mrs. Kirby and her lawyers are insufferably rude to the Vanderhof clan. In an outpouring of genuine affec-tion, Grandpa's friends pay his fine when he pleads guilty and Mr. Kirby is touched by the show of affection for one person. Alice, disgusted by Mrs. Kirby who has told her, "If you had any sense, young woman, you'd stay where you belong and stop being ambitious," tells her what she thinks of her and what she can do with her precious son. Alice then leaves town. Tony, disillusioned by his father's greed and by Alice's desertion, quits his job and goes to the Vanderhofs—he always belonged more to the free spirit world than the business world. Mr. Kirby begins to feel guilty; he realizes that while he may have great wealth, he is a poor man compared to Grandpa because Grandpa has friends who love him. Mr. Kirby goes to Grandpa's house

and winds up playing a harmonica duet with him. Mrs. Kirby
walks in on the scene and promptly faints at the sight. Alice
returns home and is reconciled to Tony, and everyone except
Mrs. Kirby seems to live happily ever after. Mrs. Kirby, trapped
in her ideas of propriety, remains stiff and unable to see the
shortcomings in her life or the simplistic joy and contentment
to be found at the Vanderhof's. Her inability to change causes
her to be left behind as both her husband and her son desert
their former life styles. Unfortunately, she did not profit from
the advice given Mr. Kirby by Grandpa when they shared a
jail cell, "You can't take it with you. As near as I can see, the
only thing you *can* take with you is the love of your friends."
Mrs. Kirby chose the comfort of money over the comfort of
friends or family, and wound up unhappy and confused; the
inherent lesson was not lost on the audience.

In summation, the scatterbrained mothers are usually mothers
in name only. They are not evil women, but they are preoccupied
with the trappings of wealth and display none of the noble
maternal attributes Hollywood emphasized in more dramatic
motherly roles. These mothers provide negative role models for
their children, who often seem to inherit the least desirable
personality traits of their mothers, especially in regard to money.
As suggested earlier, nothing is as plain as the message that
great amounts of money cause great amounts of trouble. Indeed,
for the mothers of this category, money caused so much trouble
that it even exhibited the power to overwhelm maternal instincts
and responsibilities, reducing the mothers to the status of child-
women. These are the mothers who make psychologists very
rich people.

What, then, can be concluded from these various images of
motherhood? Certainly, we can see that the movies presented
very consistent images and role expectations for older women.
Motherhood was biologically ordained and culturally required
for a woman to be properly fulfilled in life. Few options existed
for these women. Some films featured older women in non-
maternal roles: as tough prison matrons in *The Criminal Code*
(1930) and *Condemned Women* (1938); as cynical but irreplace-
able secretaries in *The Awful Truth* and *Easy Living* (both 1937),
and *Too Hot To Handle* (1938); and as unmarried women who

greatly regret their situation in *Gold Diggers of 1933, Smartest Girl in Town* (1936), and *The Awful Truth* (1937). An abbreviated look at *The Awful Truth* provides an excellent example of the type of image under discussion.

The Awful Truth starred Irene Dunne as Lucy Warrimer and Cecil Cunningham as her Aunt Patsy Adams. Lucy moves in with Patsy while in the process of obtaining a divorce from her husband, Jerry (Cary Grant). To occupy herself, Lucy dates a wealthy but naive man and convinces herself to accept his proposal of marriage. At the possibility of Lucy marrying again so quickly, Aunt Patsy (who until this time has appeared as chic, happy and contented) advises restraint, saying:

> Do you know what rebound is? That business of
> trying to get over one love by bouncing into love
> with somebody else. It's fine, except the rebound is
> rarely the real thing. As a matter of fact, it's the bunk.
> There's a first bounce, and a second bounce and . . .
> well, look at me. You'll wind up like an old tennis
> ball.

Though Aunt Patsy advises caution, the implications for a woman who never marries are presented as less than favorable. Indeed, Lucy returns to her husband, even though she is aware of his extramarital dalliances, for the sake of true love. Apparently, an unfaithful husband is better than no husband at all.

These non-motherly characters usually appear physically unfeminine—particularly the prison workers and secretaries, who are as plain in appearance as they are efficient in practice—and possess personalities that draw contempt and/or pity from the viewer rather than striking positive role models.

The majority of film mothers are portrayed as widows during this period, as if all a mother and child required for growth were each other. Other than a biologically required function of procreation, fathers are superfluous to the certified importance of the mother/child relationship. Indeed, few if any films deal with the implications of a lack of paternal involvement in a child's life in the same way they explore the problems of a motherless existence.

Aging women during this period are not, for the most part, portrayed as suffering from debilitating diseases now associated in the public mind with old age—arthritis, poor eyesight, impaired hearing, and the like; such maladies are attributed to few of the characters surveyed. Characters who do display ailments are often caricatured as hypochondriacs, older women for whom going to the doctor was as routine as any other weekly activity, a situation that usually signaled a lack of worthwhile involvement with other people and concerns.

It is certainly not from this period of filmmaking that cultural notions of older women as frail, vulnerable, helpless little old ladies emerged. In a Hollywood that glorifies the family unit, the image of mother is the solid foundation that makes the unit firm. As long as the idea of the extended family holds high cultural importance, the role of the aging mother is assured; as the family structure in twentieth century America evolved, so too did the images of older women. The images of traditional mothers, however, make infinite psychological sense during the Depression and war years.

The aging women characters are perhaps too simply portrayed, too selfless in their desire to help their children, too long-suffering in their stoic confrontations with the injustices of the world. They are, however, presented as characters to be admired more than pitied, savored more than thrust aside as anachronisms. Assuredly, a few exceptions exist—wicked old witches and cruel stepmothers appear at times (Christmas 1937 saw the premiere of Walt Disney's first animated feature film, *Snow White*, which featured one of the most despicable mother images of all time)—but these are, indeed, the exceptions.

Not found in any significant number in the popular films of the thirties and early forties are older women who have chosen to remain childless and are ultimately happy with their situation; indeed, the concept of choice has little to do with motherhood during this time frame. This is the area of concern in which the greatest shift in attitude occurs over the following thirty-five years of Hollywood films. The emergence of options for women, greatly boosted by the development of effective birth control and the legalization of abortion in the sixties, did the most to alter the images discussed in this chapter. It was to be a social revolution that Hollywood, and the American culture, would rally against for years.

NOTES

1. Adrienne Rich, *Of Woman Born: Motherhood as Experience and Institution* (New York: W. W. Norton & Company, Inc., 1976), p. 13.

2. Ann Douglas, *The Feminization of American Culture* (New York: Avon Books, 1977), p. 87.

3. Barbara Ehrenreich and Deirdre English, *For Her Own Good: 150 Years of the Experts' Advice to Women* (Garden City, New York: Anchor Books, 1979), p. 13.

4. Peter Gabriel Filene, *Him/Her/Self: Sex Roles in Modern America* (New York: The New American Library, Inc., 1976), p. 7.

5. Douglas, *The Feminization of American Culture*, p. 88.

6. It is important to note that such interpretations may partially be the result of the biases of the times in which these authors were writing, and as such, require cautious acceptance. Carl Degler points out "that though the separation of the spheres was a part of the actual lives of women in the 19th century, the practice ought not to be seen as necessarily either demeaning or unduly subordinating" (*At Odds*, p. 50). An objective viewpoint sees that nineteenth century middle-class women were sharply segregated into specific areas of activity, but whether the women themselves felt abused and restricted is a different concern. The presumed moral superiority of women was a role both men and women were socialized to accept.

7. Ehrenreich and English, *For Her Own Good*, p. 24-25.

8. Marabel Morgan, *The Total Woman* (New York: Pocket Books, 1974), p. 20-21.

9. Quoted by Filene, *Him/Her/Self*, p. 36.

10. David Wallechinsky and Irving Wallace, *The People's Almanac* (Garden City, New York: Doubleday & Co., Inc., 1975), p. 939.

11. Jessie Bernard, *The Future of Motherhood* (New York: The Dial Press, 1974), p. 12.

12. Paul Goodman and Frank O. Gatell, *America in the Twenties: The Beginnings of Contemporary America* (New York: Holt, Rinehart and Winston, Inc., 1974), p. 9.

13. Ibid., p. 15.

14. Sheila M. Rothman, *Woman's Proper Place: A History of Changing Ideals and Practices, 1870 to the Present* (New York: Basic Books, Inc., 1978), p. 21.

15. Ibid., p. 147.

16. Madeline Edmondson and David Rounds, *From Mary Noble to Mary Hartman: The Complete Soap Opera Book* (New York: Stein and Day, 1976), p. 56.

17. Ibid., p. 57.

18. Ibid.

19. Ibid., p. 33.

20. Nye, *The Unembarrassed Muse*, p. 213.

21. Ben M. Hall, *The Best Remaining Seats: The Golden Age of the Movie Palace* (New York: Bramhall House, 1961), p. 17.

22. Leslie Halliwell, *The Filmgoer's Companion* (New York: Avon Books, 1975), Fourth Edition, p. 517.

23. See Mary Daly, *Gyn/Ecology* (Boston: Beacon Press, 1978), Chapter Six.

24. Elizabeth Janeway, *Man's World, Women's Place*, pp. 126-127.

25. L. Frank Baum, a staunch advocate of the concept of the agrarian paradise, gathered many Populist sentiments and gave them literary life in *The Wonderful Wizard of Oz* (originally published in 1900). The power of the individual to direct his own destiny, as well as the disenchantment with urbanization and its overall problems, led Baum to infuse his stories with political significance. In her study of Baum's books, *Wonderful Wizard, Marvelous Land* (Bowling Green University Popular Press, 1974), Raylyn Moore observed about Oz, "it turns out that at the heart of the urban society there is fraud and deceit, that the wizard is a humbug, that their hope of salvation lies in their own internal resources as opposed to external assistance."

Also interesting for its treatment of Baum's original book as an allegorical interpretation of the Populist movement is Henry M. Littlefield's "The Wizard of Oz: Parable On Populism" *(American Quarterly*, Spring, 1964).

26. Leila Rupp, *Mobilizing Women for War*, p. 73.

27. American films of the thirties and early forties often used European settings, particularly horror films or movies dealing strongly with questionable moral and ethical codes. The European setting provided a psychological distancing for the audience, so that subjects pertaining in content to Americans could be perceived more objectively, and less threateningly, by the viewers. There was also some sense of Europe as a more decadent, more liberal atmosphere that allowed certain ideas to be explored that Americans were not ready to admit might exist in their "new land."

28. David Zinman, *Saturday Afternoon at the Bijou* (New York: Castle Books, 1973), p. 369.

29. Halliwell, *Filmgoer's Companion*, p. 468.

30. Bergman, *We're in the Money*, p. 96.

31. Bosley Crowther, *The New York Times*, 2 May 1941, p. 25.

32. "Scatterbrained" is one of those terms that, hopefully, will be heard less as times passes. However, it is used here to refer to women who seem incapable of following a logical flow of ideas, who make inappropriate mental connections, and who ultimately cause pandemonium to reign as they act, and cause others to act, on this misinformation. Gracie Allen, of the Burns and Allen comedy team, developed this particular type of characterization to its fullest expression, though Gracie's particular interpretation was somewhat more ingratiating than the women of the same general type in Depression era comedies.

3

POSTWAR FILMS:
MOM, APPLE PIE,
AND THE CRISIS NEXT DOOR

> Under patriarchal socialism we find
> the institution of motherhood revised
> and reformed in certain ways which
> permit women to serve (as we have
> actually served through most of our
> history) *both* as the producers and
> nurturers of children *and* as the full-
> time workers demanded by a devel-
> oping economy.[1]

> Motherhood affords an instant iden-
> tity. First, through wifehood, you
> are somebody's wife; then you are
> somebody's mother. Both give not
> only identity and activity, but status
> and stardom of a kind.[2]

Philip Wylie published *Generation of Vipers* in 1942 to a general critical reaction of bemusement; the sources for the problems in the world, according to Wylie, were within ourselves—
and "Mom" led the parade as the chief problem maker for her
male offspring.

    The America of 1942 was somewhat more concerned, how-
ever, with coping with the immense problems of the armed

world conflict and content to debate the causes of it after the war ended. Elementary school students are taught the fact that the American participation in World War II brought an effective conclusion to the economic uncertainties of the preceding decade; industrial production, geared to supplying munitions and military necessities, operated at full capacity and offered well-paying employment to any individual who desired the opportunity to work. The facts that are generally forgotten, or glossed over by the history texts, are the ones relating to the effect of the war on women and working, and ultimately on women and the home.

As the military commitments of the United States stretched to accommodate a war being fought on two fronts—in the Pacific and in Europe—more and more men enlisted or were drafted into the armed services. Even though young, unmarried women traditionally remained in the work force until marriage (an aftereffect of World War I), their total numbers were too few and their job skills too restricted to totally fill the void in the heavy-duty factories. A major campaign was started by the federal government to encourage all women—single and married— to work in wartime industry, and to convince them that they would be able to accomplish the work required as well as men in the same positions. Author Sheila M. Rothman points out, however, that the federal government made it abundantly clear that the full employment of women in factories was an extraordinary measure intended only for extraordinary times, "At the very time that the federal government pleaded with women to take war jobs, it made eminently clear that work for them was a temporary measure. . . . When peace returned, they were to return to their homes."[3] Regardless, the figures were impressive; the number of women who worked outside the home doubled, women witnessed a significant rise in wage scales, and female membership in unions quadrupled.[4] The official government attitude had turned one hundred-eighty degrees from the attitude of the thirties. Barbara Deckard points out:

> In the 1930s, women were told to stay in the home,
> that going to work was unnatural. Overnight, with
> the heavy demand for labor, all of the media, ad-

vertising, and government posters declared that it is
both natural and patriotic for women to work. It
was emphasized everywhere that Hitler's Germany
tried to keep women in the home for nothing but
sexual reproduction, that fascism tried to push these
sexist attitudes on the world, and that American
women must fight fascism and sexism by working in
the war economy.[5]

Rosie the Riveter became a symbol of female capability, adapt-
ability, and determination to contribute meaningfully to the
war effort.

Baxandall, Gordon and Reverby, writing on the history of
working women in this country, maintain that the involvement
of women in the industrial war effort "did not make a lasting
or profound difference in the public attitude toward women
who worked nor did it redefine the sex roles."[6] Many women
had been working for four years when the war ended, receiving
better wages than ever before, and were not necessarily ready
to abandon their measure of independence; a significant number of women—single, war-widowed, or just plain poor—were
not in a financial position to be forced back to so-called wom-
en's work of being waitresses, hairdressers, and secretaries.
Surely, a large number of women war workers (particularly
middle-class women) had seen their jobs as necessary but temporary, and were relieved to relinquish their jobs to returning
veterans so that they could marry and begin their long-postponed
families; the interpretive danger lies in believing that this desire
to end well-paying employment was held by all women workers
in 1945.

The federal government did its fair share to exert pressure
on working mothers to leave their factory jobs by eliminating
the funds that had established and maintained day care centers
during the war. With the men back in the employment picture,
the official position held that mothers no longer belonged in
the labor force.

With public and governmental sentiment firmly against them,
working women had few options. Wartime had been an excep-
tional time that had called for unusual solutions. As Rothman

says, "The war was not so much a transforming experience as an interruption, after which women returned to pursue an inherited role."[7]

The postwar period again raised a fundamental question of twentieth century life: what was the proper role for women in American culture? In the mid-forties, however, the "woman problem" had an extra dimension added to it. The war factory experience had proven women's capabilities beyond the limits of home; in the postwar period, with a variation on the standard "how do we keep them down on the farm after they've seen Paris," the question became, "how do we keep them in the kitchen and wiping runny noses after they've seen financial and emotional independence?" The answer was the same as it had been fifty years earlier—pull the pedestal out of the attic, dust it off, and reinstall it in the center of suburbia. The "gilded cage" cannot be totally condemned, however, nor can all middle-class women be identified as unwilling victims; for many women, the roles of wife and mother held the social identity they had been raised to anticipate and embrace as adults, and many were possibly quite content to leave the factory work behind to pursue more traditional roles. As Leila Rupp points out, "The feminine mystique was no new creation, but simply the 1950s version of the traditional wife and mother. The postwar image did not have to make tremendous adjustments. Rosie simply stepped out of her overalls, still wearing her apron underneath."[8] The end of the war meant lower production of war-related products; industry could not retain women workers and rehire veterans, so the women were the first to leave. Industrialized growth relied, however, on producing consumer goods; industry needed women to marry and raise children so that she and her family could provide a market for industrial products.[9] Everyone seemed to profit from this arrangement, except perhaps for the women who were at the center of the master plan. The war had redefined the world order, but American women were still expected to act out their traditional roles. The nation, physically unaltered by the ravages of warfare, desperately sought a return to psychological normality, a normality that insisted that Mom be in the kitchen, teaching the girl next door how to bake apple pies. Older women, however, did not experience the same ease of role resuming; battered

by Wylie's condemnation and confronting the suburban, nuclear family world of the postwar era, the grandmothers of
America were looking for a place in the brave new world, and
finding themselves passed by.

The postwar solution was to be found in the reinstitution-
alization of what Betty Friedan was later to label the "feminine
mystique." Women had to be reminded that certain biological
capabilities provided them with talents which could be best
explored within the context of the home. Ferdinand Lundberg
and Marynia F. Farnham (sociologist and psychoanalyst, res-
pectively) helped popularize Freudian notions of female "needs"
and repressed desires (of course, Freud had not invented these
ideas—he just provided labels for behavior which he interpreted
within a distinctly Victorian context). They felt that the female
role needed to be reinvented, and the publication of their book
in 1947, *Modern Woman: The Lost Sex*, was timed perfectly
to lend expert advice to women who ever doubted where
their real vocation in life was to be fulfilled. Consider, for
example, the following excerpts from their work:

> What woman has lost must in some way be recap-
> tured. Society must recognize her need and make it
> possible for her to satisfy her healthy ego aims with-
> out sacrificing her instinctive desire for motherhood
> or the needs of her children.
>
> . . .
>
> The problem is not only to get women into the
> h⊃me but to get them there on a basis satisfactory
> to their own feelings and aspirations.
>
> . . .
>
> If women could be *attracted* into organizing their
> lives more closely around the home and spheres of
> nurture, an important step would have been taken
> in making the home a place where children might
> grow up into well-balanced adults.
>
> . . .
>
> The psychically balanced woman finds greatest
> satisfaction for her ego in nurturing activities.
>
> . . .

Women would do well to recapture these functions
in which they have demonstrated superior capacity.
Those are, in general, the nurturing functions centering around the home.[10]

The recurring message is that a woman is most feminine and
most fulfilled when she is performing functions that make life
better and easier for other people. Certainly, as a concept, this
notion of selfless sacrifice is anathema to modern day feminists
and "me-generation" devotees; given the temper of the times,
however, it was an explanation and rationalization that was
firmly embraced and subscribed to by the middle class. It was,
after all, the way in which the majority of women had functioned in the past.

Even Dr. Spock (whose first edition of his baby book was
published in 1946) joined the ranks of those who tried to instill
guilt in women who were not disposed toward staying home
on a full-time basis. In his section titled "The Working Mother,"
he counseled:

It doesn't make sense to let mothers go to work
making dresses in factories or tapping typewriters
in offices, and have them pay other people to do a
poorer job of bringing up their children.
    The important thing for a mother to realize is that
the younger the child the more necessary it is for
him to have a steady, loving person taking care of
him. If a mother realizes clearly how vital this kind
of care is to a small child, it may make it easier for
her to decide that the extra money she might earn,
or the satisfaction she might receive from an outside
job, is not so important after all.[11]

As Philip E. Slater would explain so precisely in *The Pursuit of
Loneliness* in 1970, American middle-class women in the postwar period accepted the "Spockian challenge"—that every child
has the capability of greatness, if nurtured properly, that "in a
product-oriented society, she (mother) has been given the opportunity to turn out a really outstanding product,"[12] and

that, through the achievements of her child, a woman could realize her own creative drives.

The concept of writing a book of instruction on the proper manner in which to rear children holds, on a more subtle level, the proper manner in which mothers should act to order their own lives. Writing in the *American Quarterly* in the winter of 1977, Nancy Pottishman Weiss remarked, "In one serious sense child rearing manuals might be renamed mother rearing tracts. Behind every rule concerning desirable child behavior a message to mothers was couched, advising them on how to act and recommending the right, proper, and moral way to conduct their own lives."[13] Middle-class women were encouraged to devote their full-time energies to their children; to do less was to invite self-loathing and public disapproval.

The demographic realities of the postwar baby boom are history, but a history that the United States lives with daily. Twenty percent of all Americans now alive were born to those women who believed in Dr. Spock and migrated to the suburbs to raise healthy children. The suburbs offered sanctuary from dirty cities and problems of urbanization, but they also physically reasserted the gulf between the public sphere of men's work and the private sphere of women's homes. By actually placing women in a far-removed, country-like physical setting, the cultural delineations were powerfully reinforced.

So, the pedestal was back—but what were the audiences seeing when they went out in the evening to see a movie?

Wartime films had seen the emergence of what Molly Haskell has characterized as "superwoman—a woman who has a high degree of intelligence or imagination, but instead of exploiting her femininity, adopts male characteristics in order to enjoy male prerogatives or merely to survive."[14] Rosalind Russell's tailored suits, Joan Crawford's padded shoulders, and Bette Davis' tough-as-nails exterior were perfectly attuned to the real world of the audience in the early- and mid-1940s. The postwar time frame, however, found these roles inappropriate. How could middle-class women be convinced to stay in the suburbs if their favorite female stars were out choosing careers instead of babies and laundry? As Haskell points out, this conflict set the stage for films in the late forties and early fifties, "which tried, by ridicule, intimidation, or persuasion, to get women out of the office and back to the home."[15] The campaign to diminish the popularity of the superwoman was superbly reflected in the popular films of the time period.

An intrinsic part of the plan to reestablish ultrafemininity as the ideal model for women to follow was to dwell heavily on the idea of time, and what happens when time passes quickly and a woman suddenly discovers herself on the verge of cultural extinction at the age of forty. Perhaps the biggest change in attitude came about in the film depiction of middle-age, and the illustration of the devastating consequences it held for women who had failed to fulfill their lives by marrying and mothering. Middle age became, very quickly, a "now or never" watershed for female characters, the time that would inalterably set one's life course from that moment until death arrived to release the hold. The message was not very different from the message that had been taught in the thirties—women need children to be fulfilled—but the transmission of the message became shrewish, insistent and overly alarming. Rather than seeing older women characters who basked in the adulation of their families, audiences began to be exposed to older women who had denied themselves the traditional role and were not just unhappy about it, but in many instances actually driven insane. The audience was left to assume that craziness in women was a direct result of stubborness and self-centeredness, a refusal to live as society expected. If Hollywood could not lovingly cajole women back into their homes after the war, perhaps it could terrify them into the comfort and insularity of the suburbs by painting a vivid enough scenario of what a husbandless, childless future might hold. A number of films serve to illustrate this attitudinal transition.

The Snake Pit (1946) starred Olivia de Havilland as a bona fide patient in a state mental institution. The film is usually remembered for exposing the wretched conditions of many mental care facilities, but the movie is of particular interest for its pseudo-Freudian insights into what caused the woman's illness, and the signs that indicated that she had recovered. Olivia de Havilland portrays a married woman who suffers a total nervous collapse. After her confinement, therapy unveils

the details of her long-repressed miserable childhood—deserted
(through death) by the father she loved, neglected by her
unfeeling mother—and presumes to offer the rationale for why
she, as an adult, disliked men and domesticity with such a
vengeance. The audience is shown the seeming irrationality of
her feelings—she has a nice home and a good husband who loves
her, though they are childless—and by the end of the film she
is "cured" and well enough to leave because she has realized
that her life's happiness is to be found in a traditional domestic
role. She discovers that it is not marriage and family life that
are bad, but rather the inappropriate role models she has endured
in the inadequacies of her parents. She leaves the hospital with
her husband, leaves behind the sick women who play with dolls
all day in imitation of the maternal role they never experienced
(or, by implication, never matured far enough to accept their
maternal destiny and so remained forever childlike in their
activities), presumably to return to the suburbs and sanity.

The metaphor of houses as tombs emerges again and again
in films dealing with elderly women in the postwar period. One
such example exists in *The Lost Moment* (1947), a bizarre
story of undying love, jealousy and murder, based on Henry
James' novel, *The Aspern Papers*. Agnes Moorehead portrays
Juliana Bordereau, 105 years old, the object in her youth of a
collection of incomparable love poems written by her lover,
poet Jeffrey Ashton. Juliana lives in Venice with her niece,
Tina, in the same huge, forbidding house that she had shared
with Jeffrey. Juliana and Jeffrey had been lovers of intense
passion and international renown; all assumed that his untimely
death so many years before had turned brokenhearted Juliana
into a recluse; indeed, she had not left the house in more than
seventy-five years. Robert Cummings plays an American publisher, familiar with the correspondence between the two lovers,
who wishes to obtain the rights to it for his company. Traveling under the name William Burton, he rents a suite of rooms
in Juliana's home under the premise of completing a novel.

Burton's arrival at the house is far from warm. Niece Tina,
severely attired (though pretty), is as gloomy and cold as the
house itself. Burton's first glimpse of Juliana, a woman he
knew only through the poems, was horrifying to him: "This was

the divine Juliana of Ashton's poems," he narrated. "An ancient, hooded skull . . . old . . . old beyond my wildest expectations." The camera never shows Juliana's face, but focuses instead on her gnarled and gaunt hands, the withered flesh barely covering the bones, her fingers adorned with oversized rings that only emphasized the human deterioration. Juliana's attractiveness had been physical, and her human shell served as a reminder of how fleeting were the physical determinants of beauty for women.

Juliana allows Burton to rent rooms because she needs the money; Tina bitterly resents his presence, but bows to her aunt's wishes. It is not long before Burton realizes that some deep mystery pervades the house and the people in it. The servants are afraid of Tina. The parish priest cautions Burton not to disrupt the private world of Tina and Juliana, lest he unleash a force that could not be controlled. Hearing mysterious piano music one night, Burton follows it to a secluded part of the vast house, where he finds Tina beautifully dressed, hair combed out, believing herself to be Juliana and Burton to be Jeffrey; he plays along with her delusion. Her split personality causes her to hate and abuse her elderly aunt. Juliana, in response to Burton's questions about Tina's fantasy, tells him how she used to read Ashton's love letters to Tina as a child, and when Juliana's eyes failed her in old age, Tina began reading them aloud. Tina ultimately takes the letters from her aunt and uses them to become Juliana whenever she wishes. Tina is only alive in the past, in another woman's life; she has no real life in the present or forseeable future. Again, the parish priest feels that if Tina could fall in love in the present, she would be "cured" and no longer need her romantic delusions; toward that end, he encourages Burton's posing as Ashton.

In the confrontation scene of this suffocating melodrama, old Juliana tells Tina that Jeffrey is dead, lost to both of them because she had killed him when he threatened to leave her, and that her father had buried Jeffrey in the garden. Juliana had remained in the house all those years, protecting her secret and letting the world believe the myth of her love affair. Burton interrupts the confrontation as Tina is choking her aunt;

his voice startles Tina from a trance-like state, and he rushes her out of the room. A candle, overturned in the confusion, starts a fire, and ancient Juliana dies clutching Jeffrey's letters in her hands.

The relationship between Jeffrey and Juliana had never truly existed as he had painted it in the artistry of his poems. Tina, in a strange way, is the Juliana of the poetry and love letters. Burton goes to Venice seeking the letters, but finds something far better—a living, breathing Juliana who is in love with him. All it requires is his presence to snap the hold of her schizophrenia, to provide Tina with a real-life focus for her romantic delusions. The construction of the film allows the viewer to feel only pity for Juliana's wasted life and joy that Tina has been saved from the same lonely fate. The male, and marriage, as agents of rescue and salvation were to be seen many times over in the years to come. Women (as well as men) had been socialized to expect men to fulfill this role of protector. Simone de Beauvoir comments, "Cinderella does not always dream of Prince Charming; whether husband or lover, she is afraid he may turn into a tyrant. . . . But almost always she will attain her ambition through masculine 'protection'; and it will be men—husband, lover, suitors—who will crown her triumph by letting her share their money or their fame."[16]

Perhaps the most important lesson taught, by example, by the mothers of the fifties to their daughters would be the need to expand their options to avoid the fate of living vicariously through the accomplishments of husbands and children.

The year 1950 was not just the beginning of a new decade, but also a year that witnessed the release of three excellent films that had a great deal to say about how women should conduct their behavior to maximize emotional returns in their later years.

Harriet Craig, starring Joan Crawford in the title role, is a moral lesson to every wife who thinks it is her proper role to be the boss in her family. Harriet, the wife of a good and generous man who is very devoted to her, is an incredible shrew to everyone but her husband, whom she manipulates precisely through a smoke screen of proper devotion and sexual eagerness.

Harriet has no patience and demands the most from everyone who comes in contact with her; her talents would have been applauded as managerial genius if she had been a man, but her sex made the personality traits of decisiveness and perfectionism inappropriate. Harriet is so coldblooded and disliked by others that not even one ounce of sympathy is allowed her by the viewer.

Harriet's home bears a striking resemblance to a museum; unique pieces of furniture are arranged in precise order—everything has a function and a purpose, and she allows no deviation from her rigidly structured schedule. Harriet is so thoroughly obsessed with being the perfect wife, and ordering her surroundings to the same degree, that she manages to build her own mausoleum around her. The house is as sterile and as cold as Harriet, a perfect mirror of her empty personality.

Harriet's mother is confined to a sanitorium; Harriet visits and tries to provide company. She encourages her mother to walk in the garden, but her mother insists, "No, I have too much mending to do." In reality, her mother has no responsibilities, but she wanders mentally into a world where she has a home and a family and a purpose. The woman psychiatrist explains to Harriet that her mother has withdrawn into an escape world, to remove herself from something with which she is incapable of coping. That "something" is never clearly defined by the doctor, though the loss of function and role might be a good guess. Harriet has her own explanation, however, insisting that her mother's problems stem from the desertion of her husband when Harriet was fourteen years old. Returning home on the train after visiting her mother, Harriet talks to her cousin/secretary, Claire. The conversation was meant, obviously, to provide the audience with a dose of armchair psychoanalysis and an insight into Harriet's bruised psyche:

HARRIET: I was just thinking. I don't like trains. I don't like the feeling of being rushed along in the darkness, having no control, putting my life completely in someone else's hands.

CLAIRE: When you got married, did you feel something like that?

HARRIET: No, I didn't. But the average woman *does* put her
    life completely in someone else's hands—her husband's. That's
    why she usually comes to grief.
        Marriage is a practical matter. A man wants a wife and a
    home. A woman wants security. No man is born ready for
    marriage—he has to be trained.

Harriet's venomous hatred of her father transferred to all men;
she had to control everything within her grasp, crush all op-
position, and in the process she managed to kill the particular
brands of femininity and sensitivity so necessary to the fifties
ideal.
    Harriet tries to sabotage a promotion (that would mean
Walter going to Japan without her for three months) by telling
his boss that he is a gambler who needs her guidance and emotional support to stay honest. Walter discovers what she has
done and finally realizes what a liar and manipulator she is. At
the same time, he finds out that Harriet is capable of having
children, though she had always told him differently, and it is
this one last deception that he cannot bear. Walter's discovery
of her scheming and lying is not enough to make him leave
Harriet, but his realization that she is purposely refusing to
have a family is the one lie he cannot forgive. Harriet has allowed her self-protective mechanisms to turn her into a domineering, controlling monster; her refusal to have children proves
just how pitiful she has become.
    The baby boom reality of the fifties reinforced the need for
children as verification of a woman's true femininity; Harriet's
self-imposed sterility extended to every other aspect of her
life. As Walter leaves, the viewer finds relief in his escape from
the tomb before the seal was in place. Harriet had constructed
a world in which she could function, in which she was boss,
but she wound up ruling a world inhabited by only one person.
    Harriet's downfall was not a result of her demands that her
house be perfect and her life be ordered; her flaw was that she
chose to achieve these aims by behind the scenes manipulation
of her husband. She lost her husband because she treated him
like a fool, and because all of her actions were designed to
please and protect herself, not her husband and the children

he wanted to have. In *Harriet Craig,* self-interest was the greatest
of sins, and one that marked the sinner as unwomanly.

Gloria Swanson as the pathetic but egomaniacal old film
star Norma Desmond in *Sunset Boulevard* (1950) displays,
once again, the heavy price a woman pays for vanity and
childlessness. A review of the film in *The New York Times*
calls the Swanson character a "wealthy, egotistical relic, desperately yearning to hear again the plaudits of the crowd."[17]
Norma Desmond is a relic, a living piece of the past whose life
has no relevancy to the present. The past exists only in her
mind, but it is a past in which she had ruled Hollywood as one
of its finest silent film stars. Living in a decaying mansion,
attended by faithful servants who support her fantasy by writing
and mailing fan letters to her on a weekly basis, Norma plans
to return to her career, a return to "the millions of people who
have never forgiven me for deserting the screen."

To stage her return, Norma hires a young, cynical and financially adrift screenwriter named Joe Gillis; Norma insists he live
in her house, where he quickly assumes the additional role of
gigolo. Norma and Joe's first conversation quickly sets the
mood of the movie:

JOE: You're Norma Desmond. You used to be big.

NORMA: I *am* big. It's the pictures that got small.

Gillis easily assesses his new boss: a woman "still waving proudly
to a parade that had long since passed her by."

Throughout the film, the audience is bombarded with the
fact that Norma's total existence is a shakily constructed fantasy based on her stardom many years before; her mansion is
crumbling around her, a mockery of the splendor it had once
known, just as Norma is crumbling physically, the distance
between her fantasy and her reality becoming greater and
greater. Norma's entire world is in a kind of time warp, a place
where time has not been allowed to move on. Explaining to
Gillis that "great stars have great pride," Norma surrounds herself with photographs that stand as mute testimony to her
former success; she submits to endless cosmetic procedures in
a quest to preserve the flesh that had made her famous.

As the movie progresses, it becomes more and more difficult
to distinguish between Norma the woman and Norma the actress; all of her actions are exaggerated to the point that everything becomes a scene to be choreographed, blocked and played
out. Norma plays so many scenes that the real woman she must
have been at one time disappears in a shadow of affectation.
Susan Sontag has written that:

> To be a woman is to be an actress. Being feminine
> is a kind of theatre, with its appropriate costumes,
> decor, lighting and stylized gestures. From early
> childhood on, girls are trained to care in a patho-
> logically exaggerated way about their appearance
> and are profoundly mutilated by the extent of the
> stress put on presenting themselves as physically
> attractive objects.[18]

Norma Desmond is consumed by her narcissism, a narcissism
that society had sanctioned and encouraged for her in her youth
but which has turned into a cruel farce with the onset of age.
Norma's appearance is her identity; she dismisses sound films,
saying, "We didn't need dialogue; we had faces then," and she
lives her life like some silent melodrama, orchestrating her
movements and facial expressions into an exaggerated and grotesque imitation of life. Norma's dilemma is best described by
Simone de Beauvoir, who observes:

> Long before the eventual mutilation, woman is
> haunted by the horror of growing old . . . to hold
> her husband and to assure herself of his protection
> . . . it is necessary for her to be attractive, to please;
> she is allowed no hold on the world save through the
> mediation of some man. What is to become of her
> when she no longer has any hold on him? This is
> what she anxiously asks herself while she helplessly
> looks on at the degeneration of this fleshly object
> which she identifies with herself. She puts up a battle.
> But hair-dye, skin treatments, plastic surgery, will
> never do more than prolong her dying youth. . . . But
> when the first hints come of that fated and irrevers-

ible process which is to destroy the whole edifice
built up during puberty, she feels the fatal touch of
death itself.[19]

Gillis tires of his life with Norma and unable to stand the
humiliation of being deserted, Norma kills Joe. When the murder is discovered, police and newsreel crews arrive at the mansion.
By this time, Norma belongs totally to her fantasy; she believes
the gathering crowds to be her fans, just like the old days, clam-
oring for a glimpse of their favorite star. Max, the butler (who
had been a silent film director and the first of Norma's three
husbands), has "directed" Norma's life for years, making sure
she never notices the passing of time. As Norma descends the
grand staircase, to the police and newsreel cameras waiting
below, Max stands amid the camera crew, verbally directing
Norma's final scene. It is a fantasy life that filmgoers would
encounter again in the early 1960s, in Bette Davis' performance
in *Whatever Happened to Baby Jane?* The insistence that aging
women conform to socially sanctioned age role expectations
which significantly restrict their options and activities raises a
problem of great proportion for all women. Negative stereotypes
of aging dehumanize women who are already old, and threaten
younger women rather than challenging or comforting them in
their aging process. Given the social realities of the fifties, who
(in the final analysis) can really blame Norma Desmond? The
blame belongs squarely on the shoulders of the "Feminine
Mystique".

Joe had once told Norma, "There's nothing tragic about
being fifty, unless you try to be twenty-five." Unfortunately,
Norma never learns to act any other way; she is totally un-
equipped to mature, and when her flesh can no longer support
the lie, she has nothing left but insanity. She is the epitome
of superfemininity, but she fails to make the transition to wife
and mother, to "settle down," at the appropriate time in her
life. This failure is her flaw, and once again the sins of selfishness and self-interest come to a grievous conclusion. The fact
that this film premiered at Radio City Music Hall, a theatre
which prides itself on always providing entertainment suitable
for family viewing, underscores the audience for whom the

moral lessons were intended and at whom they were aimed.

A 1950 film that carries basically the same message as *Harriet Craig* and *Sunset Boulevard* but delivers it in a somewhat more palatable form is a vehicle for Bette Davis, *All About Eve.* This film is an exploration into the bitchy, gossipy, backbiting world of the professional theatre. It is a story of survival and a story of female competitiveness; it raises, and answers, the female dilemma of the postwar period—career versus marriage.

Margo Channing (Bette Davis) plays the leading female star of Broadway, a cynical but oddly attractive personality with a gigantic ego and an acidic tongue. She is forty years old and at the peak of her career, but suddenly she must contend with a rising starlet in the person of Eve Harrington (Anne Baxter), a cold and calculating opportunist who fools everyone into believing that she is a meek and humble fan. Margo hires Eve as her secretary, taking pity on her after Eve relates a phony, but thoroughly convincing, tale of woe. Margo's friends all see Eve as a paragon of virtue and industriousness, which alerts Margo's jealousy and causes her to begin to mistrust Eve's motives. Margo is envious of Eve's youth, and threatened by her presence, particularly when Eve is named her understudy for the play "Aged in Wood." The play title is appropriate for Margo—she is tough and hardworking and has earned her fame. It is equally appropriate for Eve, whose sweet exterior conceals an insatiable ambition that allows nothing, and no one, to stand in her way. Eve is, indeed, a schemer and manipulator; Margo had been right in her instincts to feel threatened all along. Margo, talking to her friend, confides that she has finally realized that the bottom line for happiness is having a husband and a family, not a career:

> Funny business a woman's career. The things you
> drop on your way up the ladder—so that you can
> move faster—you forget you'll need them again when
> you go back to being a woman. That's one career all
> females have in common whether we like it or not.
> Being a woman. Sooner or later we've got to work
> at it, no matter what other careers we've had or
> wanted. And in the last analysis nothing is any good

unless you can look up just before dinner—or turn
around in bed—and there he is. Without that, you're
not a woman. You're something with a French pro-
vincial office—or a book full of clippings. But you're
not a woman. Slow curtain. The end.

Eve manipulates her way to stardom, but the audience knows
full well that her reign will be relatively short, lasting only until
another ambitious woman emerges in the years to come to
challenge Eve for her position.

When Margo utters the famous line, "Fasten your seat belts,
it's going to be a bumpy night," she expresses only too well
the trouble to be encountered by women who are ambitious.
The movie places two determined women in a cutthroat competition with each other, but the loser of the fight, Margo, is
actually the winner in the eyes of the audience. The attitude
is clearly expressed that her choice of family over fame will
serve her far longer than if she stumbled on as another Norma
Desmond, refusing to believe that the past was gone forever.
Eve, victorious in her career, would be successful only until
the next good actress came along; Margo, the audience senses,
has accepted the greatest role of her career—wife and mother.

Postwar Hollywood had not forgotten Philip Wylie, nor had
it dismissed the accusations he had hurled at "Mom". Wylie's
writings about the devastating consequences of Momism were
not particularly conducive to convincing middle-class women
of the joys and rewards of motherhood in the late 1940s, and
few films risked their potential female audience by blaming
maternal characters for psychologically destroying their children;
this was a phenomenon that would begin to appear on American
screens in earnest by the 1960s.

One film of the postwar period that did attempt to provide
an example of Momism, however, was *Come Fill the Cup* (1951),
starring James Cagney as Lou Marsh, an alcoholic reporter.
Brilliant but troubled, Marsh loses his job, his girl and his
health to alcoholism; he winds up in the gutter, but is hospital-
ized and recovers. Determined to live his life sober, he returns
to the newspaper as a stock clerk and rises, in five years, to the
position of city room editor. Lou believes in rehabilitating

alcoholics, and hires a number of ex-drinkers as reporters. Seeing
that Lou is successful in his one-man rescue attempts, the paper's
publisher summons him to straighten out his nephew, Boyd
Copeland (Gig Young), a young man who is ruining his health
and wasting his talent with alcohol.

Lou unhappily assumes the task of helping Boyd. The audience knows that Lou is tough but fair, and that he is a good
reporter with a trained eye for detail and the ability to get
quickly to the center of a problem. Consequently, the audience
can only believe Lou when he identifies Dolly Copeland, Boyd's
hysterical mother, as Boyd's biggest problem. Dolly hovers
over her only child as if he were totally helpless; when he is
sick with a hangover, Dolly moves into Boyd's room to be with
him, exiling his young wife to a different wing of the house.
In one particularly revealing scene, Boyd returns home drunk
and rambling incoherently; Dolly comfortingly reassures him
that "It's all right, darling, Mother knows; it's all right." Lou,
witnessing the interaction between mother and son, interjects,
"Leave him alone, Mrs. Copeland. You're smothering him."
After Dolly and Boyd leave the room, Lou talks to the publisher:

LOU: Did it ever occur to you to keep her out of it?

PUBLISHER: After all, Lou, she is his mother.

LOU: Maybe that's why he's on the bottle.

Boyd had been a promising composer, but is now unable to
finish any piece of music he begins to write. A huge oil painting of Dolly hangs on the wall overlooking Boyd's piano in
his apartment; the mother character is obviously blamed for
Boyd's emotional, intellectual and physical decline. Her dedi-
cation to her son has turned into his psychic castration.

Boyd's drinking begins to cause real trouble; he ultimately
angers a professional hoodlum, who engineers a car accident
which Boyd walks away from but is fatal to his passenger.
Genuinely shaken by the accident, Boyd stops drinking and
accepts help. The publisher sends Dolly on an extended world

cruise. Boyd removes the oil painting of his mother, and is mirac-
ulously able to complete his concerto in record breaking time.
When Lou questions the removal of the portrait, Boyd explains,
"It was like working in a pressure cooker." Dolly, then, was the
source of endless conflict for her son; he could only mature
when she was physically removed from his life.

The character of Dolly was genuinely despicable; not even
her love for Boyd could redeem her smothering techniques to the
audience. A word of caution went out to the audience—be a
good mother, but temper your motherhood with restraint.
Motherhood must be selfless, a role to fulfill the needs of the
child, not dwell on the needs of the mother. The image of
mothers such as Dolly would emerge fully by the end of the
1950s, as the audience demographics shifted and new messages
were called for. Commenting on the radical change in attitude
toward the mothering role, and the transition from "mother"
to "Mom," Jessie Bernard points out that "less than halfway
through the present century this monument of love, sacrifice,
tenderness had become a viper."[20] The viper images would
become more obvious as time moved on.

The postwar period, then, was a time of reestablishing "normality," of attempting, as a nation, to recover from a conflict
that had radically changed the world. It is not surprising that
American popular culture would attempt to restore the pedestal
of motherhood—nurturing, devoted, loving Mom—as a means
of reasserting the value structure the country had always relied
on. For all the reasons previously outlined—both real and
imagined—the country needed middle-class women to be solidly
rooted in the home, and it needed the movie images to reinforce
the importance of this need. If, however, "the middle-class is
the most fertile breeding ground for the growth of Momism,"[21]
as Hans Sebald contends in *Momism: The Silent Disease of
America*, then the makings of an anti-Mom epidemic in the
1960s were already in the works. Momism was a particularly
harsh indictment of older women, a mid-century indictment
of a generation of women who had come to late middle-age
during a time of fundamental change in the styles of living
and working common to the majority of the population. Greater
leisure time was available, but no one had trained people how to

use it effectively or productively. Jessie Bernard makes an excellent argument that these women were born into, and socialized through, a Victorian social system that no longer held any relevance in the world they found themselves in fifty or sixty years later.[22] These older women became as obsolete in the modern era as the buggies they had ridden in as children. Bernard aptly describes these women as victims rather than villains, an assessment which becomes more obvious over time.[23] The problem for the fifties and sixties, however, would be in the "Mom" stereotype which had developed, a negative image which promised to far outlive its appropriateness. The culture returned to the image of Mother to heal its war-related wounds, but for the first time in the twentieth century, the image was tarnished. Motherhood now had the capacity to be a negative as well as positive role, a situation which began the decline of older women in the popular mind from contributing, functioning members of society to useless relics.

The lessons women had learned about themselves and their capabilities during the war were not forgotten; they were, however, put on a dark shelf for the 1950s, to find their way out through another generation of women—the daughters of "Mom"—in the 1960s and 1970s.

NOTES

1. Adrienne Rich, *Of Woman Born*, p. 54.
2. Betty Rollin, "Motherhood: Who Needs It?" *Look Magazine*, 22 September 1970.
3. Rothman, *Woman's Proper Place*, p. 222.
4. Barbara Deckard, *The Women's Movement* (New York: Harper and Row, 1975), p. 301.
5. Ibid., p. 303.
6. Rosalyn Baxandall, Linda Gordon and Susan Reverby, *America's Working Women* (New York: Vantage Books, 1976), p. 281.
7. Rothman, *Woman's Proper Place*, p. 224.
8. Leila Rupp, *Mobilizing Women for War*, p. 175.
9. Baxandall, et al., *America's Working Women*, p. 283.
10. Ferdinand Lundberg and Marynia Farnham, *Modern Woman: The Lost Sex* (New York, 1947), pp. 363-367.

11. Benjamin Spock, *The Common Sense Book of Baby and Child Care* (New York: Duell, Sloan and Pearce, 1946), p. 484.

12. Philip E. Slater, *The Pursuit of Loneliness* (Boston: Beacon Press, 1970), p. 67.

13. Nancy Pottishman Weiss, "Mother, The Invention of Necessity: Dr. Benjamin Spock's *Baby and Child Care*," *American Quarterly*, Winter, 1977, p. 520.

14. Haskell, *From Reverence to Rape*, p. 214.

15. Ibid., p. 222.

16. Simone de Beauvoir, *The Second Sex* (New York: Bantam Books, 1968), p. 534.

17. "Sunset Boulevard," reviewed in *The New York Times*, 11 August 1950, Section 15, p. 2.

18. Susan Sontag, "The Double Standard of Aging," reprinted in *The Older Woman in America*, p. 16.

19. Simone de Beauvoir, *The Second Sex*, p. 542.

20. Jessie Bernard, *Women, Wives, Mothers*, p. 138.

21. Hans Sebald, *Momism: The Silent Disease of America* (Chicago: Nelson Hall, 1976), p. 41.

22. Jessie Bernard, *Women, Wives, Mothers*, p. 140.

23. Ibid.

4

AGING AS CRISIS:
THE OLDER WOMAN
IN THE 1950s

> My mother is soothed at last by her
> television, watching lives much more
> professional than ours.[1]

The 1950s were a time of structural upheaval for Hollywood studios. A number of factors joined forces to significantly alter the role that movies played in the lives of the American public.

Radio and movies had always managed to coexist peacefully; the former offered intimate immediacy and the latter provided a visual fantasy world. The rapid emergence of television in the postwar period, combining the best elements of radio and film in the home, wreaked havoc with movie attendance figures and helped precipitate a major realignment of the film industry. Television was a gimmick, a novelty, but one that was destined to become an American necessity. Television, however, cannot be blamed entirely for Hollywood's troubles.

The antitrust legislation against movie studio ownership of theatres came to a negative conclusion for Hollywood; in 1948, the Supreme Court ordered an end to the monopolistic practices of the studios in relationship to film distribution. The end of block booking meant the end of a guaranteed distribution policy for all films produced, regardless of the quality of the product. With declining attendance and unsure markets, the era of mass production of popular films came to a halt. With

less production, the studio system became bulky and expensive
to maintain, so that it, too, was virtually dead by the early 1950s.

Hollywood spent the fifties attempting to rediscover their
audience. The eighty-seven million people who had once attended the movies every week turned their allegiance to the ever-
growing television industry. This wholesale desertion of Hollywood by a significantly large percentage of the population
produced a shock that Hollywood did not rebound from until
the sixties. The sixties would bring forth a new demographic
grouping to frequent the theatres, and Hollywood would finally
realize that its profits were to be made by acknowledging and
fulfilling the tastes of specialized audiences rather than mass
audiences. All the old rules were antiquated by 1950; it took
ten years for Hollywood to discover what the new game con-
sisted of, and how to write a game plan that would turn the
contest to its advantage.

Television, the darling of the fifties, knew nothing but rapid
growth, public acceptance and guaranteed profits. To grow so
quickly, and please so many, television relied on the same stories
and the same character types that the mass popular audience
recognized so well from radio and film entertainment of the
preceding decades. This continuity of images was absolutely
essential to a new medium attempting to ingratiate itself to as
many potential viewers as possible. Consequently, no entertainment on television was uniquely designed for the new
medium; TV relied on the standard formulaic situations and
stereotyped characters for its success.

Though film images of aging women had begun to change
by the late forties, no such problem existed for TV producers.
The older women, particularly the mothers who had comforted
and reassured film-goers for years, found a new home on the
smaller screen. Indeed, many of the same characters made a
successful transition from radio and/or the movies to television.
Gertrude Berg moved *The Goldbergs* to television in early 1949,
winning an Emmy Award for Best Actress in 1950,[2] and continuing on the air until late 1954. Molly Goldberg was a gossip
and a meddler, but in a manner that endeared her to her family
and neighbors. In 1961, Gertrude Berg returned in a series
entitled *Mrs. G. Goes to College*,[3] which followed the misad-

ventures of a Jewish grandmother returning to school (in 1961,
a somewhat unusual situation). Between radio and TV, America
watched Mrs. Goldberg age over a period of thirty years.

A second transitional program was entitled *The Aldrich
Family*, which had been a radio and "B" film series. Running
from 1949 until 1953,[4] it presented its particular brand of
small town life, with aging Mrs. Alice Aldrich planted firmly
in the kitchen.

A TV spin-off of the radio favorite, *Fibber McGee and Molly*,
was *Beulah*, a situation comedy about a black domestic who
was constantly saving her ridiculous white employers from
themselves. Aired from 1950 until 1953,[5] *Beulah* is easily recog-
nizable in the 1980s version of *Benson*, which features a black
butler who is far more intelligent than the governor who employs
him; Benson carries the heavy burden of covering the governor's
mistakes so that the voters do not realize that a bumbling idiot
is in charge of the state government.

Any number of older mothers-in-law and landladies populated
the middle-class situations of early television. Spring Byington
as Lily Ruskin kept *December Bride* on the air from 1954
until 1961.[6] Lily was the perfect model of the ideal mother-
in-law—she never meddled with her daughter's family, causing
her to be loved by all. Vivacious and outgoing, she showed that
neither widowhood nor advancing age were in themselves reasons
to retire from an active life. *My Friend Irma* (CBS, 1952-1954),[7]
a radio transplant, followed the story of the title character, a
dumb blonde of classic description, who lived in older Mrs.
O'Reilly's boardinghouse, where most of the story took place.
My Little Margie, a vehicle for Gale Storm from 1952 until
1955,[8] saw Gertrude Hoffman as elderly neighbor Mrs. Odetts,
who enthusiastically helped Margie implement any number of
crazy schemes. Elderly Mrs. Davis (Jane Morgan) was the landlady to Eve Arden on *Our Miss Brooks* (CBS, 1952-1956),[9]
another radio transplant, and perhaps one of the most memorable situation comedies ever to appear on television. *Young Mr.
Bobbin* (NBC, 1951-1952)[10] was a comedy that followed the
life of a young man who lived with the two elderly aunts who
had raised him, one quite organized and practical, and the other
eccentric and bubble-headed. His aunts were forever complicating

his life, particularly his attempts at romance. This particular
format would appear again as *Bringing Up Buddy* (CBS, 1960-
1961),[11] except that both aunts on the later show were flighty
but well-meaning.

Perhaps one of the most memorable early television programs
was *Mama*, based on the play and movie, *I Remember Mama*.
The character of resourceful and kindhearted Mama was played
by Peggy Wood, who managed to endear the portrait of an
immigrant mother guiding her children by traditional values
to the hearts of millions of viewers. Mama was the perfect embodiment of the good mother, self-sacrificing and devoted, who
was so familiar to film audiences of the thirties and forties.

Mothers-in-training had many TV role models in the middle-
aged maternal characters who were so necessary to the domestic
comedies of the fifties. Whether it was Harriet Nelson playing
herself on *The Adventures of Ozzie and Harriet* (ABC, 1952-
1966),[12] Jane Wyatt as Margaret Anderson on *Father Knows
Best* (1954-1963),[13] or Barbara Billingsley as June Cleaver on
Leave It To Beaver (CBS, 1957-1958; ABC, 1959-1963),[14] a
solid portrait of middle-class domestic life riveted itself in the
minds of those who viewed, and established standards of home
life by which people would judge their own families. Television
mothers always wore stylish dresses and frilly aprons with no
spots in sight, and they always managed to produce warm
cookies and cold milk at the sound of a footstep on the back
porch. These women were superfeminine but sexless, servile,
and ultimately superficial. They were women who made careers
of homemaking, and they left a legacy of indelible images on
young viewers who would grow up only to find themselves in
a much different world.

Prime-time programs did not stand alone in their reenforce-
ment of standard images of older women. The TV soap opera,
providing the staple of afternoon programming in the fifties,
became, by the late seventies, the most consistently successful
and profitable of any regularly scheduled programs. Older wom-
en on soap operas have always fallen into two general categories,
the good grandmother and the meddlesome grandmother. Both
types of women act out of genuine concern for their families,
but the first is wise and respectful of her adult children and the

second is misguided and often portrayed as attempting to
perpetuate decidedly un-American notions of social class distinctions. Good grandmothers on soap operas are, to this very
day, women very much like Ma Perkins of the early radio serial.
They have no genuine problems of their own, and serve primarily
as guidance counselors for the young and confused people
around them. The meddlesome grandmother is neither evil nor
deliberately destructive, though she is often scheming and
manipulative; her only redeeming quality is that she genuinely
believes that her family needs her intercession, and acts out of
some peculiar standard that convinces her that the end justifies
the means. Soap opera story lines specifically show the audience
which of the two types of older women is the acceptable model;
the good grandmother is rewarded by her special place in the
family as well as the devotion of all who know her, while the
meddlesome grandmother is continually frustrated in her attempts to choreograph the lives of her children and very often
suffers serious repercussions (in the form of anger and rejection
on the part of her children) from grand schemes that backfire.
Ironically, the meddlesome grandmothers seem to generate
more viewer enthusiasm than the good grandmothers, perhaps
because they act outside of social expectations of appropriate
behavior for older women.

Television in the fifties, then, assumed the thankless task of
trying to please all the people all the time, and film concen-
trated on its strengths to lure people out of their comfortable
living rooms and into neighborhood theatres. Movies, compared
to television, had the obvious advantages of both color and
larger-than-life screen size. The controlled access to movie theatres, however—that is, that people had to buy tickets to enter,
and the management could refuse to sell tickets to people based
on age—made it possible for filmmakers to begin to explore
sexual topics in manners far more revealing than in previous
years. What Marjorie Rosen has labeled "Mammary Madness"[15]
seemed to overtake Hollywood products, and titillating sex
appeal became the casting order for the day. The popularity
of Marilyn Monroe—who, in retrospect, was as much a gifted
comedienne as a sexpot—encouraged any number of dumb,
blonde, big bosomed imitators. The renewed emphasis on

physical beauty—at, many would argue, the expense of sensu-
ality—also made older women all the more obvious losers in
the flesh game presented on the screen. American movies in the
fifties passed through a schizophrenic time in terms of presenting women; a woman was either a sex object and center of
adolescent fantasies, or the girl next door (Debbie Reynolds,
Doris Day, Audrey Hepburn) who was also a center of adolescent fantasies, though somewhat subdued. Each type was searching, ultimately, for the one thing that guaranteed happiness
and success—a husband. In her perceptive study, *On The Verge
of Revolt: Women in American Films of the Fifties*, Brandon
French chronicles the cultural denial experienced by women
during this all-important decade, suggesting that the tranquility
and domesticity often attributed to the fifties were, indeed,
the germinating seeds for the feminism of the sixties and seventies

> On the surface, fifties films promoted women's
> domesticity and inequality and sought easy, opti-
> mistic conclusions to any problems their fictions
> treated. But a significant number of movies simul-
> taneously reflected, unconsciously or otherwise,
> the malaise of domesticity and the untenably narrow
> boundaries of the female role. By providing a double
> text, which contradicted itself without acknowl-
> edging any contradiction . . . they documented the
> practical, sexual, and emotional transition women
> were undergoing beneath the threshold of the con-
> temporary audience's conscious awareness.[16]

Three films exhibit interesting responses to middle-aged
women characters, each in a somewhat different plight, but all
searching for the male companionship that would give fulfillment to their empty lives. *All That Heaven Allows* (1955) is the
story of widow Carrie Scott (Jane Wyman) and her love for a
man who is both younger than she and her social inferior, Ron
Kirby (Rock Hudson). Carrie is a lonely woman when the
audience meets her; her two children are away at college and
she is at loose ends, emotionally and socially. Her friend suggests
buying a television set to help pass the time, but Carrie resists

because of its symbolic presence as a passive companion for people who are alone.

Ron, a nursery owner, is a quiet man of few words, a person who would easily qualify for the label of rugged individual. The audience is reminded on several occasions that "to thine own self be true" is Ron's creed and that Thoreau is his mentor. Carrie's loneliness overcomes her sense of social propriety and allows her to become friendly with Ron; they fall in love and want to marry, but her children are obnoxious and her friends are contemptuous and rude. Many of the sneers and objections revolve around intimations of sexuality; Ron, a younger man, certainly desires sexual relations, an idea treated as unseemly for a woman Carrie's age (which is, at the outside, forty-five). Her son snaps at Carrie, "I think all you see is a good looking set of muscles . . . haven't you any sense of obligation to Father's memory?" Not wishing to upset her children, Carrie breaks the engagement, choosing her children's welfare over her own happiness.

Months pass; at Christmas, Carrie's unhappiness and loneliness are emphasized by the joy of the holiday, and she realizes that she made the wrong choice. Her daughter announces her intention to marry and her son is going to Paris to study for a year. As a Christmas gift, her children present Carrie with a television set; the delivery man promises "drama, comedy, life's parade at your fingertips," but Carrie sees only her own reflection in the empty screen, her own life passing by.

Carrie begins to develop severe headaches; her doctor, a close friend, tells her the cause of the pain is her unrequited love for Ron, and the only sure cure is marriage. The doctor, a male voice of authority, helps to convince Carrie that she has nothing to lose by going to Ron, and a life of happiness to gain. Before she can be reconciled to him, Ron suffers a semi-serious accident, which brings Carrie rushing to his bedside. And as the violins swell, the viewer is content that Carrie has at last found the place where she belongs.

All That Heaven Allows has a number of conflicting messages for middle-aged women. On the positive side, women were being told that self-sacrifice was not necessarily the rewarding prospect that it was previously displayed to be, particularly when no one benefited from it; women—and men—were also being told that older woman/younger man liaisons were neither unnatural nor impossible. (This is a message which has not really implanted itself in the popular consciousness even today, regardless of the practical aspects of the arrangement in terms of male/female longevity. The film's focus is on social class and rank, concerns to suburban audiences in the fifties. If remade today, the older woman/younger man issue would be paramount, reflecting social concerns of the eighties.) On a more negative note, Carrie never sought outside activities to assuage her unhappiness and relieve the emotional burden of her widowhood. Having spent her entire adult life as a wife and mother, she had only those roles to rely on in her search for new happiness, and only her position as Ron's wife would make her life once again complete. Ron's desire to live in the country and be self-sufficient did, indeed, remove Carrie from the suburban lifestyle and "empty nest" maternal role; it did not, however, release her from the traditional sex role nor really encourage her mental development as a woman who could rely on herself and be happy. Carrie would still function as a wife and homemaker and would still find true contentment only in a traditional marriage situation. As a whole, however, *All That Heaven Allows* (soap opera that it was) revealed more stirrings of female self-determination than most of the films produced in the same era. Even in acknowledging that, however, one of the strongest messages of the film was a familiar one: a woman could only find lasting fulfillment and happiness in the traditional role of wife, caring for the needs of her man.

Joan Crawford forged her career by portraying tough women who possessed drive and ambition and became, as a consequence, a caricature of femininity who could only be redeemed by heroic gestures (as in her award winning portrayal in *Mildred Pierce*, where she willingly confesses to a murder committed by her daughter, to save her child from going to jail). We of another era look back upon Crawford as an emancipated ideal, but for the times in which she lived, she was an ambiguous characterization. One Crawford film in which she portrayed the lonely widow seeking love was *Female on the Beach* (1955). Crawford played the part of Lynn Markham, the wealthy widow of a professional gambler who had taken her out of a chorus line in Las Vegas and had initiated his young wife in the "ways of the world." In middle-age, she was tough and cynical, a force to be reckoned with. Visiting a beach house owned by her dead husband and which she intends to sell, Lynn meets Drummond Hall (Jeff Chandler), a handsome gigolo who preys on lonely widows. Initially, Lynn wants nothing to do with the man or his obvious overtures; she recognizes him for what he truly is, and knows enough to avoid contact. Drummond is persistent, however—after all, it is his livelihood—and some mysterious quality about him begins to draw the widow into deliberate rendezvous with him.

In Drummond Hall, the viewer is confronted with a heavy dose of brutal Momism. He has a deep, jagged scar on the side of his neck, which he self-consciously fingers whenever he talks about women. He tells Lynn, "I don't hate women. . . . I just hate the way they are," and comments, "Women—they're not soft and they're not gentle." The viewer soon discovers that he lived in an orphanage from the age of ten, and that the scar on his neck was the remnant of a knife wound inflicted on him by his mother, just before she killed herself. This explanation is offered as the total rationale for his brooding, menacing, unromantic attitude toward women. In a fit of anger brought on by remembering his mother, Drummond physically abuses Lynn and then engages in sexual intercourse with her ("making love" had nothing to do with the act, and it fell somewhat short of rape). Suddenly, the hard-bitten, world-seasoned Lynn is transformed into a giddy school girl, pacing through the house all day and hanging on the phone, praying that he will call and ask to see her again. Her life and her plans are totally dropped in the hope that the virile young man will not desert the middle-aged widow, now portrayed as nymphomaniacal.

Drummond does fall in love with Lynn and marries her, though soon after she suspects that he intends to murder her for her money. The viewer is not sure what to think, so vividly has the film painted the picture of Drummond as woman-hater. As it turns out, another woman who was in love with Drummond and jealous of Lynn had plotted to kill her. Drummond turns out to be safe and protective after all, transformed by the real love of a woman who would not hurt him. The fear and distrust felt by Lynn toward her new husband, regardless

of how satisfactorily it was resolved, is part of what Andrea
Walsh has identified as a sub-genre of suspicion towards men
that was very present in American films in the postwar period.
In what she calls the "culture of pain," Walsh sees, "a female
mode of defensiveness and suspicion (that) has often co-existed
with a more dominant ideology that stressed love, support and
nurturance of the 'right man.' "[17] The ambiguity of Drummond's
personality caused intense confusion and fear for Lynn, who
was not at all certain that her instincts had not failed, allowing
her to marry a man who not only might not love her, but
might wish her bodily harm.

In Crawford's portrayal of Lynn Markham, there exist a
number of conflicts and contrasts. She claims not to need love,
and yet she dissolves quickly and grasps it readily when it is
offered. She seems to be independent, and yet willingly deserts
that stance to submit to Drummond, a man who tells her, "A
woman is no good to a man unless she's a little afraid of him." The
viewer ends up with the same message that *All That Heaven Allows*
taught in a more gentle manner: that a woman is incomplete
without a man, that true love ultimately forgives any number
of transgressions and solves most problems. The desperation is
particularly acute for aging women, eager to grasp any relationship (even one that is frightening or dangerous) rather than be
left behind. A more disturbing element exists within *Female on
the Beach*, however, and that is the message that even though
men and women need each other to fulfill their lives, the two
sexes never really understand the motivations that push each
other toward their destinies. And that kind of relationship is a
disaster looking for a place to happen.

On a crying scale of one to four handkerchiefs, *An Affair to
Remember* (1957) clearly ranked a five. A story of feminine
self-sacrifice and genuine love, it tells the tale of two people
who fall deeply in love but almost lose the opportunity to
make a life together. Terry McKay (Deborah Kerr) meets Nicky
Ferrante (Cary Grant), international playboy, on a ship headed
for America, where each of them has a fiance waiting. As fate
would have it, they fall in love but Terry resists because she
feels obligated to the man who is waiting for her.

Making a port call in France, Nicky takes Terry to meet his

ancient but spirited grandmother (Cathleen Nesbitt, who would
play a very similar role on the television series, *The Farmer's
Daughter* from 1963 until 1966)[18] who lived alone, almost
cloistered, in a villa on a cliff overlooking the harbor. The
grandmother likes Terry a great deal, encouraging her attraction
to Nicky by confiding, "There is nothing wrong with Nicolo
that a good woman couldn't make right." Terry is so taken
with the elderly woman that she changes her mind, realizes
that she is in love with Nicky, and that she will only be happy
marrying him. Terry and Nicky decide to meet again in six
months, on the top floor observation deck of the Empire State
Building, if they are free to marry. Both have to break off
their respective engagements, and learn how to support themselves financially. Terry returns to her supper club singing career,
and Nicky (a talented painter) paints houses to reorient himself to the idea of working for a living. The big day arrives and
Terry, hurrying to meet Nicky, is struck by a car directly in
front of the huge skyscraper. Thinking she no longer loves him,
and unaware of her accident, Nicky returns to Europe and his
grandmother's house—though she had died in the interim—and
begins to paint seriously. Terry, badly crippled, teaches music
in an elementary school, but refuses to even attempt to contact
Nicky unless she can be a "whole woman" again. Nicky returns
to New York, and they see each other at a ballet performance.
He tracks her down to her apartment to demand an explanation
of why she did not keep their appointment. He delivers a hand-
made shawl that his grandmother had wanted her to have, but
almost fails to discover her medical problem until it dawns on
him that she has not moved from the couch since his arrival.
He begins to talk about a painting he had done of Terry and
his grandmother, explaining that his dealer had told him that
a crippled woman had purchased it. Searching the apartment,
he finds the portrait hanging in Terry's bedroom, and realizes
the reason she had not come to him.

Nicky's grandmother had been the tie between the two lost
lovers. Their pride had stood in their way, but the gentle intercession of the grandmother who loved both of them was enough
to save the relationship. As Terry was leaving the grandmother's
house, she said she would like to stay forever because of its

beauty and serenity. Grandmother, wise and loving, replied,
"You are too young for that, my dear. It is a good place to sit
and remember but you still have to create your memories."
Nicky's grandmother represented traditional values and mores,
a simple style of living that the two young people had lost sight
of before they met each other. She was the embodiment of a
happy, contented old woman who had lived her life for her
husband and children and who, at the end of her life, had no
regrets or unfinished business. She is the same older woman
who has always existed in American film, and she helped reinforce the need for women to marry and domesticate themselves.
She best serves to illustrate the fact that not all aging images
in the fifties were negative reinforcements, that the images
that had been established in the thirties and early forties co-
existed with the shrill and frightening aspects of aging that
emerged in the postwar period.

The fifties were not the carefree, silly years that nostalgic
television programs such as *Happy Days* and *Laverne and Shirley*
would have us believe. They were years of surface banality,
with important cultural changes fermenting underneath. It was
a decade that found its ultimate symbol of youthful vitality
in the election of John F. Kennedy to the presidency in 1960,
and a decade that was psychologically jolted into the next era
by his assassination in November of 1963.

It is becoming increasingly obvious that the fifties were not
just years of transition, but years in which the social, psychological, and political theories of the preceding fifty years came to
fruition. America's psychic wrestling with the McCarthy witch
hunts, the Cold War, the rise of rock 'n roll, the growth of television, and the threat of "the bomb" (among other traumas),
provided cultural stress and strain that would explode in the
innumerable movements and "isms" of the sixties. For the
subject at hand—the images of aging women in American popular film—it was a decade of important attitudinal changes:
changes that would allow us to actually pinpoint the development of negative ideas about growing older, and changes that
would explode on the screen in the sixties in the grotesque and
pathetic images of women in films such as *Whatever Happened
to Baby Jane?*, *Hush, Hush Sweet Charlotte*, and *Psycho*.

The fifties were the years in which old age became a part of a woman's life cycle to be avoided, physically and mentally, and the time that middle age began to turn into a period of crisis. No woman could look forward to aging because she was too consumed by the grief she felt over the passage of her youth. Biological determinants of youth for women, sexual attractiveness and procreative abilities, became more than mere parts of a total woman, they became the elements that were absolutely essential to save women from the loneliness and frustration sure to accompany a husbandless or childless old age. Certainly, films during the fifties still portrayed a significant number of the types of older women encountered in previous decades; the stereotypes were far too ingrained to disappear completely. The significance is that the first real deviations in these portrayals began to appear with some degree of frequency during a time that the culture, as demonstrated earlier, was very much in need of perpetuating traditional sex roles, yet chose to do so through negative rather than positive reinforcement.

Margo Channing's admonishment to her guests in *All About Eve* to "Fasten your seat belts, it's going to be a bumpy night," was an instruction well-suited to the film portrayal of all women in the fifties. For older women, as portrayed in film, the ride in the sixties was going to get a great deal worse before it got any better.

NOTES

1. Maureen Howard, *Bridgeport Bus* (1966), quoted in Elaine Partnow, *The Quotable Woman* (New York: Anchor Books, 1978), p. 401.

2. Tim Brooks and Earle March, *The Complete Dictionary to Prime Time Network TV Shows, 1946-Present* (New York: Ballantine Books, 1979), p. 772.

3. Ibid., p. 225

4. Ibid., p. 17.

5. Ibid., p. 60.

6. Ibid., p. 152.

7. Ibid., p. 426.

8. Ibid., p. 427.
9. Ibid., p. 468.
10. Ibid., p. 697.
11. Ibid., p. 86.
12. Ibid., p. 12.
13. Ibid., p. 196.
14. Ibid., p. 343.
15. Marjorie Rosen, *Popcorn Venus*, p. 282.
16. Brandon French, *On The Verge of Revolt: Women in American Films of the Fifties* (New York: Frederick Ungar Publishing Co., 1978), p. xxi.
17. Andrea Walsh, "Films of Suspicion and Distrust: Undercurrents of Female Consciousness In the 1940's," *Film and History*, February 1978, p. 1.
18. Brooks and March, *Prime Time Network TV Shows*, p. 195.

5

IN THE WITCH'S CASTLE: THE OLDER WOMAN IN THE 1960s

I am exactly in the middle of my life.
This is my last ascending summer.
Everything else from now on is just
falling downhill into my grave.[1]

The beginning of the sixties brought something to Hollywood that the film industry had been searching for throughout the fifties—an audience. The first children of the postwar baby boom, born in 1947, entered the sixties as adolescents. Raised on television, this group shifted its allegiance to films as both an integral part of its social ritual, and as a source for more explicit treatment of subject matter than television programs could provide.

Social standards were to be questioned ceaselessly as the decade pushed on. Perhaps the one most significant, indeed potentially revolutionary, change came about from the successful development of effective contraception for women in the late fifties and early sixties. For the first time, at least in theory, women had the opportunity to be sexually expressive people without the inhibiting fear of undesired pregnancy. Naive of the harmful effects of oral contraceptives that would be discovered in the seventies, the birth control pill was a scientific development that precipitated radical attitude changes. The growing availability and acceptability of birth control for un-

married women meant that women had the ability, if they
chose to exercise it, to be sexually active outside of the traditional marital structure; women had the possibility of delaying
marriage, or not marrying at all, without having to deny themselves sexual relations. Indeed, even women who chose to marry
could easily postpone children indefinitely or remain childless
for life. Certainly, the availability of contraception and all its
implications did not automatically signal public acceptance.
Old, well-established cultural mores do not die quickly or
gracefully, regardless of how inappropriate they become in
new eras. As William L. O'Neill commented in *Coming Apart:*

> One reason feminism was always taken lightly was
> that to take it seriously opened up dreadful possi-
> bilities. What if feminine equality was incompatible
> with marriage and the family? Nobody could be sure
> it wasn't. That was why even moderate feminists
> had always been viewed by some as potential home-
> wreckers. To confront the woman question squarely
> meant taking risks. Feminism might well be the most
> truly radical proposition of them all, one that threat-
> ened to reach into secret and intimate places which
> politics had scarcely touched before.[2]

Images of aging and family structure are clearly aligned; one
great fear that young people have about growing older is that
they will experience loneliness.[3] The idealized notion of family,
with the presence of children and grandchildren, not only holds
out the promise of a focus for one's energies and a guaranteed
source of constant love, but more importantly, keeps away the
fears of being old and alone. The films to be discussed within
this chapter stand as a series of musings, for a young audience,
about what life might be like if an individual did not follow
the traditional pattern of marrying and raising a family. At first,
in the early part of the sixties, the images were frightening and
scary, pictures of degeneration and human misery, reinforcing
the old messages of what an individual should do to avoid a
similar fate. As the decade moved toward the seventies, however,
certain films began to thoughtfully explore the meanings of

aging for both men and women. Indeed, as the movie audience
of the early sixties moved into an awareness of their own march
toward early middle age in the late seventies, the film images
became more and more sympathetic. Liberal objections to
sexism, ageism and racism were more increasingly reflected in
the films offered to the public as the seventies drew to a close.

It is significant that the sixties and seventies saw so many
films produced that dealt specifically with aging as a major
theme, a topic seldom approached in earlier films as either a
direct issue or a principal story line. This serves to reinforce
the belief that aging, which had turned into a cultural bugaboo
in the fifties, was an intriguing topic to the specialized film
audiences of the sixties and seventies. Somewhat as a moth is
drawn toward a flame, or as crowds form at accident scenes
to witness the gore and be relieved they were not involved, so
did young audiences approach the inevitable but almost incom-
prehensible condition of their own aging and the mysteries
within that condition.

The definition of aging also took on new significance as the
sixties progressed. As noted in chapter four, middle-age became
a period of crisis for a woman, measured particularly by whether
or not she was married and a mother. By the early seventies,
middle age had become a crisis period for men as well as women,
and measured more in terms of self-fulfillment than in terms
of traditional social expectations.

Closely paralleling the images of decay and self-destruction
in *Sunset Boulevard, Whatever Happened to Baby Jane?* (1962)
reiterates the damage people can do to themselves and each
other when they choose to allow the past to govern their entire
lives. Baby Jane Hudson (Bette Davis) had been a popular child
vaudeville star; her plainer sister, Blanche (Joan Crawford),
had suffered through a childhood of emotional abuse and neglect as their parents did everything to advance the career of
spoiled and disagreeable Jane. As adults, the situation turned
completely around—Blanche was the star of Hollywood in the
thirties and Jane was an alcoholic has-been. From some reserve
of compassion or responsibility, Blanche always made sure
that Jane had work as an actress. One night, on the way home
from a party, Blanche was hit by a car and crippled for life;

Jane, too drunk to recall the accident, was blamed for the ruin
of her sister's career and life.

As the story moves into the sixties, the viewer finds Jane
and Blanche living in the house they had purchased many years
before, a house in such disrepair that it is literally falling down
around them. Blanche, confined to a wheelchair, is cared for
by Jane, but even in old age, their relationship remains the
same—Blanche long-suffering and Jane intolerably bitchy. Jane
is a frumpy version of herself as a child, still wearing matted
finger curls tied with limp bows, thick pancake makeup with
garish red lipstick—a grotesque version of the Baby Jane doll
that her father sold after each vaudeville performance.

Blanche is virtually imprisoned by Jane, who constantly
devises new ways to torment her reclusive sister. Jane allows
Blanche's pet bird out of its cage, and then serves it to her for
dinner. As if that were not enough, Jane adds insult to injury
by removing a dead rat from a trap in the basement and serving
it to Blanche, carefully garnished on a bed of tomatoes. After
discovering the rat and recoiling in horror, Blanche frantically
twirls in a tight circle in her wheelchair; photographed from
above, it is obvious that Blanche is as much caged as the bird
had been, and as badly trapped as the dead rat had been in the
basement.

Deciding to institutionalize Jane, Blanche tries secretly to
sell the house. Discovering the plan, Jane decides to make a
comeback, to re-stage her old act for Las Vegas and television.
This pathetic fantasy is highlighted by the obese mama's boy
she hires to serve as her musical accompanist, Edwin Flagg
(Victor Buono); Edwin's mother, who scrubs floors to support
him, coddles the lazy slob as if he were Beethoven. Edwin's
mother insists that he is a serious artist who must be spared
the more mundane aspects of the world, such as working for
a living. Edwin functions in much the same way as the gigolo
in *Sunset Boulevard*—he exploits money from a ridiculous old
woman by feeding her vanity.

Jane becomes more cruel in her determination to isolate
Blanche; she removes the telephone extension from Blanche's
room, intercepts mail and visitors, and makes Blanche afraid
to eat for fear of being poisoned. Jane is, indeed, a dastardly

person, but there is a pathetic air about her that saves her from being perceived totally as a monster. Instead, she's seen as a somewhat sympathetic character. Hearing her sing her old songs in an imitation of a child's voice only emphasizes how totally consumed Jane is by the success of her childhood, and how incapable she is, emotionally and mentally, of dealing with adulthood. Jane just cannot get out of the past long enough to catch up, and deal effectively, with the present.

Jane murders Elvira, the occasional housekeeper who had been sympathetic to Blanche. Edwin, snooping around the house in Jane's absence, discovers Blanche gagged and tied in bed, and departs in haste. Jane, fearing the police will discover Elvira, takes Blanche and drives to the beach, where Blanche finally confesses that Jane had not been responsible for the accident: "I made you waste your whole life thinking you'd crippled me. You didn't do it, Jane; I did it myself. Don't you understand? I crippled myself. You weren't driving that night . . . you were too drunk. I wouldn't let you drive." As the truth unfolds, Blanche confesses that she had tried to kill Jane. Jane, drunk, managed to jump out of the way, and Blanche crashed head on into the gates in front of the house, snapping her spine. Jane, who has appeared listless throughout the confession, responds only by saying, "You mean . . . all this time we could have been friends?" Jane reverts totally to childhood; her odd behavior draws a crowd as well as the police. Jane thinks the people are her fans, and she begins to dance to entertain them. As in *Sunset Boulevard*, the final scene presents a woman totally reclaimed by the glories of her past, glories that had effectively ruined any adult happiness.

Blanche and Jane are both pathetic characters. Crippled, Blanche chose to exercise a terrible revenge on Jane for all the inequities of the past; Blanche, too, was motivated completely by her history rather than her present. Ultimately, Blanche's revenge served only to deny fulfillment to both of them. Neither ever experienced the comforts of husband or family; each allowed the vanities of past careers to defuse other potential sources of contentment. At the end, all that remains is an overwhelming image of waste and self-destruction, and a renewed sense of just how fragile human life can be.

Two years after the commercial success of *Whatever Happened
to Baby Jane?*[4] Bette Davis had another opportunity to portray
an old woman victimized by her past and denied a normal life
by the lies of people seeking revenge. *Hush, Hush Sweet Charlotte* starred Davis as Charlotte Hollis, an old Southern belle
trying to keep her run-down mansion from being bulldozed
for a new bridge and road. Like *Whatever Happened to Baby
Jane?*, *Hush, Hush Sweet Charlotte* opened in the past, in the
time of Charlotte's youth in 1927; she was in love with a married man, John Mayhew, who ended up murdered in the gazebo
during a gala party at Charlotte's home, his head and hand
neatly severed with a meat cleaver. Charlotte is accused but
never convicted of the crime, and has lived as a recluse ever
since, taunted by local children who perpetuate her legend.

In the present, Charlotte is wealthy but unwilling to relocate
to a new home; as in other movies, the house is dilapidated, a
physical symbol of a style of life long gone. Charlotte asks her
cousin, Miriam Deering (Olivia de Havilland) to come from
New York and help her ward off the state demand for the house.
Miriam, a successful public relations executive, had been raised
with Charlotte after the death of her own parents, but she had
always been treated as second best to Charlotte and had grown
up very resentful of her inferior status in the family. It is not
long after her arrival before the bitter antagonisms between
the two women rise to the surface. Miriam, acting out of jealousy,
had told John Mayhew's wife, Jewel, and Charlotte's father
about the affair, setting off the chain of tragic events that had
led to John's brutal death. Charlotte had never really forgiven
Miriam for her interference.

Charlotte had never really accepted John's death. She still
dressed as if she were a young belle awaiting the arrival of her
beau. In her old age, she was a pathetic example of arrested
emotional and mental development. She played the harpsicord
in the middle of the night, singing the love song John had
written for her, and longing for the lover she had lost so many
years before. Charlotte never moved from the house so as to
protect her father's memory; she had always believed that he
had killed John in a furious rage over the affair. In addition,
Charlotte did not want to leave the house because it was the

only place that John still existed for her, the only place that could support her fantasy that he would one day return.

Miriam evilly plans to drive Charlotte insane, in hopes of being given control of the family money as the only surviving relative. Her plans, so meticulously enacted, almost work; Charlotte, however, hears Miriam gloating about how she had been blackmailing Jewel Mayhew all those years because she had seen Jewel murder John. When Jewel's money runs out, Miriam decides to wrest control of the family fortune from Charlotte. Jewel had murdered her own husband, and Miriam made Jewel and Charlotte suffer for it all that time. Miriam, acting out of jealousy and childhood slights, had destroyed her cousin's life. Charlotte, overhearing this story, crashes a huge cement flower urn on Miriam from the balcony above, which kills her instantly. Miriam's revenge had ultimately been the agent of her own death. Upon hearing of Miriam's death, Jewel Mayhew suffers a severe stroke and dies the next morning.

Charlotte is taken away by the authorities, to live in an institution. Physically, she appears regal, and leaves the house with her dignity intact. She had been loyal and protective all her life, and suffered for years for a crime she never committed. The similarities between *Whatever Happened to Baby Jane?* and *Hush, Hush Sweet Charlotte*, both directed by Robert Aldrich, are many, and the end result is the same—a life that never had a chance to be lived is wasted. Neither film did a great deal to reassure people that old age held the potential to be a rewarding time, a time to enjoy the benefits gathered over a lifetime. Instead, the pervasive smell of decay permeated everything it came in contact with.

Hollywood has often produced films about itself, about the misunderstood trials and tribulations of rich but unhappy movie stars. One such attempt in the sixties was *Inside Daisy Clover* (1965), literally a rags-to-riches-to-neurosis story of false values and greedy people. The setting is 1936; fifteen year old Daisy Clover (Natalie Wood) lives in an old trailer on Angel Pier with her slightly daft mother, "Old Chap" (Ruth Gordon). Daisy operates a concession stand selling autographed pictures of movie stars, while Old Chap wears big bows in her dyed red hair, dangles a long cigarette holder from her lower

lip, and reports the disappearance of her husband after seven
years because she "didn't start missing him until this morning."
Old Chap is forgetful and wanders mentally, but she is harmless
and loved by Daisy. She is, however, far removed from any
portrayal of motherhood encountered before, for she is dependent on her teenage daughter not only for financial support
but also for maintaining some mental connection to reality;
the parent/child roles are completely reversed, perpetuating
the myths of senility and "second childhood" as inevitable
components of the aging process.

Daisy has aspirations to be a singer; she makes a demonstration
record in a boardwalk booth, mails it to a movie studio, and
within days a long black limosine drives up to the pier to speed
her away to stardom at Swan Studio. She is done over, and
done in, by the studio attempts to turn her into "America's
Valentine." The studio insists that Old Chap be institutionalized
so as not to cause any embarrassment to Daisy's public image,
particularly since Old Chap's philosophy of life consists of the
belief that "this world is a garbage dump, and we're just the
flies it attracts." Daisy is both unhappy and confused about
the treatment of her mother, but is powerless to object; she
visits her mother regularly, but Old Chap becomes more quiet
and withdrawn with each passing day. Finally, the studio
chief forbids Daisy to go to the sanitarium (providing the audience's perception of him as a cold, unfeeling monster who would
separate a child from her mother), for fear that someone will
recognize her.

After a series of utter disasters—an abortive marriage with
the studio's handsome leading man who turns out to be bisexual
with a marked preference for boys, an affair with the autocratic
and manipulative studio chief, and growing dissatisfaction with
her life—Daisy tries to establish some sense of balance by taking
Old Chap out of the hospital and setting up a home with her
in a beach house. By this time, however, Old Chap has lost all
touch with reality; the loss of Daisy had also meant the complete loss of her ability to cope and function. Daisy returns
from work one evening to find Old Chap dead in bed, her playing cards blown all over the room.

The death of her mother is Daisy's greatest loss. Just as
Daisy had been Old Chap's touchstone with reality, so too had

Old Chap been Daisy's touchstone with her own past. Daisy suffers a total nervous collapse, and lies motionless and speechless in her bed for several weeks. The studio insists, finally, that she return to work. Instead, she goes into the kitchen, turns on the gas, goes out on the beach, and watches the frame house explode from a distance, laughing all the time. When asked by a passing fisherman what had happened, Daisy replies, "Someone declared war," and the audience leaves, assured that Daisy had made the right choice.

The story of *Inside Daisy Clover* is silly at times, but it manages to present negative images of aging in a vivid manner. Old Chap's elderly friends on the pier are almost as odd-acting as she; their concerns are with the zodiac and fortune-telling cards, not concerns connected to getting along in the real world. Old Chap had obviously been an eccentric woman all her life, but her unorthodox ways led seemingly to senility and lonely death. The film not only gave Hollywood studios a bad image, but reinforced aging stereotypes to a young audience of impressionable people.

In 1968, *Rosemary's Baby* was released as a kind of psychological thriller, or what Renata Adler described as "a fantasy of the What could have happened to me while I was asleep sort, What did I do when I was drunk, How do I know I'm awake now, What if everyone is lying to me. . . . "[5] Rosemary Woodhouse (Mia Farrow) and her husband, Guy (John Cassavetes), move into a spooky old apartment house which carries a bad reputation from a reputed group of devil worshippers and baby eaters who lived there at the turn of the century. As luck would have it, the rumors were well-founded, and the building is indeed inhabited by a coven of witches, all well beyond sixty years of age.

Guy and Rosemary move directly next door to Minnie (Ruth Gordon) and Roman Castevet, the leaders of the Satanic group. Minnie is extremely flamboyant, sporting heavy makeup and loud clothes; she is overly inquisitive, even asking the prices paid for furniture—she is exactly the kind of neighbor everyone likes to avoid meeting in the hall. In return for guaranteed success in his acting career, Guy allows the devil to impregnate Rosemary (which was a great deal for Guy, but a less attractive prospect for his Omaha-bred wife). The scene in which the devil rises from hell, all green and scaly, to bed Rosemary, finds all the elderly coven members in nude attendance, their sagging breasts and bent bodies in startling contrast to Rosemary's firm and youthful form. The contrast is successful in intensifying the ugliness and evil of the devil, and this is the point at which all the negative connotations connected with old age in this film come to fruition. The coven is a group of supposedly normal old people—doctors, writers, housewives—who just happen to worship Satan, and prey on young innocent women to achieve their unholy ends. The only young person who goes along with their plans is Guy, but he acts out of intense greed and selfishness, not from any belief in their philosophies.

Rosemary's Baby is a waking nightmare for the young protagonist, and the inherent comments about old age need no elaboration. The images of benevolent, harmless old people that audiences were so accustomed to seeing were totally obliterated in this modern horror tale. All the old fairy tales that pictured old women as witches had come true.

Three particularly vicious portrayals of Momism made it onto the neighborhood screens in the sixties: *Psycho* (1960), *The Anniversary* (1967), and *Wild in the Streets* (1968).

Psycho, a film in which the viewer is never quite sure if Alfred Hitchcock is playing a big private joke, is less a film of physical violence (though what violence exists—especially the graphic bathtub stabbing of Janet Leigh—is enough to ruin any appetite) than a film of intense psychological violence, of the strange workings of distorted minds.

Norman Bates (Anthony Perkins) lives with his possessive, domineering mother and runs the Bates Motel, an old motor camp that had fallen on hard times when the new highway took a different route. Norman's life is strictly controlled by his mother. He regularly runs up to the creepy house on the hill overlooking the motel, from which we hear the detached arguments he engages in with his mother. We hear Mrs. Bates objecting to Norman eating dinner with a young lady who has stopped at the motel, and accusingly shrieking at Norman, "And *then* what, after supper—music, whispers? . . . Go on, go tell her, she'll not be feeding her ugly appetites with my food or my son!" The true horror is that Mrs. Bates has been dead for years and Norman has assumed her personality in addition to

what little personality he possessed independently of her. In
The Movies on Your Mind, Dr. Harvey R. Greenberg applied
his psychoanalytic talents to unraveling Norman, and discovered
a complex situation of guilt and loneliness.[6] Though Mrs. Bates's
death may or may not have been at Norman's hands, his panic
at losing her presence was extreme. Dr. Greenberg elaborates:

> Norman came to find existence equally impossible
> with or without his mother, hated her for dominat-
> ing him, loathed himself for his crippling dependen-
> cy. . . . He did not exhume Mother out of remorse
> . . . but primarily out of loneliness, to recreate the
> demeaning protections of the symbiosis and maintain
> the nursery illusion of external sustenance if only
> Mrs. Bates could be preserved. How many nights had
> he lain on that indented bed, clutching her corpse?
> As the years passed, "Mother" grew more crazily
> oppressive and possessive. . . . The young women
> who stumbled upon the motel and aroused Norman,
> Mother ruthlessly eliminated to keep the precious
> union intact. Norman executed Marion and the other
> girls in an altered state of consciousness: each mur-
> der was a symbolic rape-revenge against his seductive,
> rejecting mother, as well as an abortive, brutal dis-
> engagement from her for which she, not he, would
> take the blame.[7]

Norman's role as mama's boy led ultimately to Norman's
psychic death. At the conclusion of the film, Mrs. Bates has
overtaken him completely, has totally destroyed the child she
once gave birth to. Instead of the nurturance mothers are sup-
posed to provide their children, Mrs. Bates had systematically
destroyed her own flesh, her power so terrible that she was able
to exercise it even from the grave. As Greenberg points out, "He
is a zombie, the marrow of his ego sucked dry by the same
mother he has (possibly) slaughtered, gutted and stuffed. Caring
and closeness have everywhere degenerated into prying and
preying." [8]
   The Anniversary (1967), though produced by Britain's Ham-
mer Films (a company best recognized for its horror productions

in the sixties), deserves some discussion because of its star, Bette
Davis (as evil Mrs. Taggart). She was the emasculating mother
of three sons; her husband, a well-to-do contractor, had been
dead for ten years. One son is a transvestite, the second is married to a woman not unlike shrewish mom herself, and the third
is a playboy who constantly brings home new girls (whom
mom dismisses just as consistently). Mrs. Taggart wears an eye
patch, having lost her eye when her transvestite son, still a child,
shot an air pistol directly into her face, shouting "Bang, you're
dead, Mummy." As the movie wears on, and Mrs. Taggart
becomes more unbearable, one can only lament the lack of
bullets in the young boy's gun!

Mrs. Taggart had a possessive hold over all three sons, financially and emotionally. Every year, the family met to celebrate
the occasion of mother's wedding anniversary, though she had
always hated her husband. The billboard copy for the film read:

> A few days ago, the whole family got together to
> discuss what to do for Mom for Mother's Day.
> Taking into consideration her love, demeanor, the
> way she brought us up, the way she accepted our
> sweethearts, the fond memories, the happy house . . .
> WE DECIDED TO KILL HER![9]

At the end Mrs. Taggart, planning the next year's celebration,
is using a small replica of "the pissing boy" (equipped with water
that sprays forth from the statue's genitals) to soak the room
and its occupants—letting everyone know exactly how she feels
about them.

The film itself bordered on high camp, but the figure of Mrs.
Taggart was all too horrifying to dismiss. She was not an example of smother love, but rather an example of a woman who
lived only for herself and cared little for the children she had
physically mothered. No one could ever accuse her of maternal
sentimentality. She was not just a bad mother, which in many
instances can be excused or at least understood; she was a
monster who had spent her life destroying people who had the
misfortune to get in her way.

Wild in the Streets (1968) was a film produced by American
International (a low budget company that had always been

quick to exploit popular culture trends in its films—a kind of *National Enquirer* approach to filmmaking) as a futuristic exploration of the "generation gap." It is a film which is probably more insightful than it was ever intended to be, showing the logical extension of cultural ideas carried to the extreme.

Shelley Winters (who has renewed her career by playing obnoxious older women) portrays Mrs. Max Flatow, a stereotyped Jewish mother who covers all the furniture with plastic, wears chin straps to bed to halt the effect of gravity, and constantly exhorts her young son to be "neat, neat, neat." Her son, Max Jr., leaves home and eventually becomes very successful as a rock singer who wields considerable power among the teenagers who comprise his national audience. Mrs. Flatow sees Max on TV and after comparing the screen image to an old family picture, squeals with the delightful thought that her now-rich son will provide generously for her for the rest of her life, if she can only be reconciled to him. She goes to one of Max's concerts, and bullies her way into his entourage. She drives away with Max in his Rolls Royce, she at the wheel; driving irresponsibly, she kills a small child. Outraged, Max banishes her from his sight, though she still basks in his reflected fame.

Max has a genuine mother problem—he hates her—and a genuine age problem—he does not want to live beyond the age of thirty. Exploiting his political base of teenagers, Max becomes president of the United States. He establishes thirty as the age of mandatory retirement, and decrees that at thirty-five, all must go to "rehabilitation camps" where they are perpetually "mellowed out" by the forced ingestion of LSD-laden water. Max's thugs, much like Hitler's storm troopers, patrol the streets looking for old people. Max's mother, a long time holdout, is carried away screaming, protesting "No, I'm young, I'm young." It soon starts to dawn on Max that as he continues to age, he will soon be old enough for his own rehabilitation. The last shot of the film shows a group of young children, angered by Max, vowing, "We're gonna put everyone over ten out of business."

Max's initial antagonism toward aging is established by the bitchy and ridiculous demands of his mother, and the apparent inability to stop her exhibited by his father. It is a film that presents "mom" as a strong factor in any boy's life, whether he accepts or rejects her values; she is the one influence that can never be entirely excised from one's consciousness.

Wild in the Streets, on a broader level, poses interesting questions about aging and cultural perceptions of the process, though it never quite manages to answer them. What is "old?" At what point are people no longer useful or contributing members of society? It underscores just how ridiculous it is to establish a chronological age to accommodate the innumerable variances in the aging process. The film, though at first glance terribly dated by its heavy dose of late sixties music and language, expresses some ideas that are still viable today and, in retrospect (regardless of the smothering mother depiction) was one of the first popular movies to consciously address itself to those concerns generated by changing cultural nuances.

The situation of older women in film in the sixties was not without its comic relief. One example exists in *Rosie* (1967), which saw Rosaline Russell reincarnate the vibrant personality of Auntie Mame as wealthy Rosie Lord of Pasadena, California (home of the Rose Bowl, football, and a peculiar brand of West Coast Americana). The film ultimately labors to present a life-affirming conclusion, but indulges in upsetting melodrama to reach it. Rather like television shows that offer a moralistic lesson but still manage to interject considerable amounts of sex and violence within the body of the program, *Rosie* leaves one wondering if a happy conclusion justifies the means through which it was achieved.

In *Auntie Mame* (1959), the middle-aged title character proclaimed "Live, live, live! Life is a banquet and most of you poor suckers are starving to death." The initial message of *Rosie* is the same. Rosie is an elderly widow who refuses to sit home and vegetate; she drives her Ferrari at breakneck speed, takes ballet classes with small children, and believes strongly in the value of vigorous exercise. Rosie tells her granddaughter, Daphne (Sandra Dee), "I'm just beginning to find out what fun life can be in my old age. It's sad, Daphne. We spend our lives learning how to live and then, just as we begin to know a little something about it, they finish us off. They ought to give us three chances, like a ballplayer." Rosie admonishes her two middle-

aged daughters to "Be in the world, and of the world, and never
say 'no' to anything."

Rosie's daughters, Edith and Mildred, are stuffy and greedy;
Rosie's husband had left his entire estate to Rosie, to the great
unhappiness of the children. Rosie provides generously for
them—giving each $100,000 each year, tax free—but they are
anxious to have it all. They decide to try to get Rosie declared
legally incompetent, and hire detectives to follow Rosie and
record her behavior. Rosie's major problem is one of age-
appropriate behavior; her activities are unacceptable because
she is elderly. Daphne, Rosie's kindred spirit, overhears the
plan and moves out of her parents' home because her mother,
Edith, is so unfeeling. Edith does not understand why her plans
should come between herself and Daphne; she is unable to apply
the lesson to her own position, to recognize that she will be
old one day as well.

The daughters have Rosie kidnapped, drugged, and taken to
an isolated rest home; she is terrified, with no idea where she
is or why. To make the situation even more pathetic, it is her
birthday. She finally learns that Edith and Mildred are responsible for her confinement, which sends Rosie into a deep depression, "And so I've come to this. So unloved, so unwanted."
Daphne and Rosie's lawyer discover Rosie's whereabouts, and
literally break her out of the rest home. Court proceedings are
enacted to ascertain Rosie's mental condition, and her depression saps her of any will to defend herself. As she explains,
"What a fool I was to believe I could start living again. But it's
gone now, finished. . . . Up until now, I thought I would like
to live forever. I think now that I've lived too long." During a
court recess, her lawyer is able to reawaken Rosie's spunk, and
she goes back into the courtroom and proves just how competent
she is. The story ends well, with Rosie's daughters exposed as
ungrateful, callous and greedy, and Rosie's vengeance complete.
Rosie proves that in movies (indeed, in most popular culture
stories), justice always triumphs; Rosie Lord had to win because
she was a fighter with a noble purpose—to "live." But Rosie
had money, powerful friends and people who loved her. What
of the older women who are poor, friendless and without people
who even know they exist? These are the women we do not

meet in *Rosie*, and these are the women who bear the greatest risk of suffering abuse and/or neglect because they are power- less. *Rosie* makes the audience feel good—evil people are justly punished and virtuous people amply rewarded. If a character of Rosie Lord's strength could be spirited away and broken psychologically, however, what could happen to the woman with virtually no defense mechanisms to come to her rescue? The images of aging presented in this film are often positive; the problem with the film is inherent in the attitude that older people cannot be victimized unless they go along with it, that they can maintain their independence if they are willing to fight for it. The movie reduces a complex set of circumstances to a simplistic argument of right versus wrong, and in so doing allows younger people in the audience to remain unaffected and unconcerned.

Mothers and daughters in conflict with each other's values was a theme to be repeated in *Rachel, Rachel* (1968), starring Joanne Woodward as Rachel Cameron, a middle-aged virgin school teacher and Geraldine Fitzgerald as her clinging and demanding mother. Rachel and her mother live on the second floor of a house that serves also as the location of the local funeral chapel; it is an appropriate location, for it signifies the death that Rachel exists within. The opening scenes of the movie provide a tour of the small town in the early morning; Rachel's alarm rings, awakening her as she lies in bed with her hands clasped one over the other, as if in her coffin. Rachel constantly carries on conversations with herself, inventing a friend who chastises and belittles her empty statements:

RACHEL: God, but I want to leave this school.

VOICE: No, you don't. If you wanted to leave, you'd leave. You'll never leave anything, Rachel.

Rachel teaches and cares for other people's children, having little of her own that is permanent, other than her love/hate relationship with her elderly mother. Rachel's mother presents an image that the daughter does not want to emulate—chin strap to reduce wrinkles that long ago decided to stay, wire

hair rollers covered by a pink net, playing solitaire until Rachel
gets home—but it is an image Rachel does not know how to
avoid.

The relationship between Rachel and her mother is the same
as it has always been; Rachel has never made the transition
to adulthood, symbolized by her unwanted virginity at the age
of thirty-five. Rachel is lauded by her mother's friends as the
perfect daughter, but they base their assessment on the fact
that Rachel is totally subservient to the demands of her mother
and has no life of her own beyond the school where she teaches
and the house where she is imprisoned. Her mother lives a life
devoid of significance as well, but in a role that is socially
acceptable for her age and widowed status.

A fellow teacher and friend, Calla (Estelle Parsons), encourages Rachel to attend a religious revival with her at the Tabernacle of the Risen and Reborn. Rachel cannot handle the
repeated exhortations to "love," so foreign is the feeling to her
and so artificial the situation in the Tabernacle. She keeps
flashing back to herself as a child, as if she and the child are
the same, with no difference in time or attitude or experience.
Calla tries to comfort Rachel, and kisses her fully and passion-
ately on the mouth; Rachel pulls away in confusion, not able to
acknowledge love from any source.

An old school friend, Nick, returns to town to visit his
parents; he dates Rachel, and they have sex, she for the first
time. Significantly, they make love in the woods, away from
the suffocating town that threatens to enfold Rachel permanently. Returning home, her mother is unhappy with Rachel's late
arrival, and Rachel fantasizes about shoving a handful of sleeping
pills down her mother's throat. Rachel's exhilaration at surrendering her virginity—"Does it show? Can a miracle happen
and never show?"—is dampened by the cool response of her
mother, and her resentment at the fact that her mother would
disapprove of her adult activities. Indeed, this is borne out
after Rachel's second encounter with Nick, when she returns
home to an irate mother, who is brandishing an old douche
bag Rachel had found in a closet and used, accusing Rachel of
immorality as if she were a naughty teenager rather than a
grown woman. Her mother's presence becomes more and more

oppressive to Rachel, who thinks to herself, "She watches the street like a captain watches the sea—praying for a funeral to come by and cheer her up."

Nick leaves town; Rachel believes she is pregnant, and is happy about the prospect of having her own child to raise. Even her baby, however, was "dead"—she had, in reality, a uterine cyst that produced signs of pregnancy—and her joy at being pregnant was reduced to part of her fantasy world; nothing could grow or prosper in the town. Rachel's experience moves her to act; after the operation to remove the cyst, she informs her mother that she is moving to Oregon (a free, open wilderness) to teach, and that her mother may join her if she wishes:

MOTHER: I don't want to move, Rachel.

RACHEL: Then don't.

MOTHER: You know I can't be left alone.

RACHEL: Then come with me.

MOTHER: Doctor doesn't want me to exert myself.

RACHEL: All you have to do is get on a bus.

MOTHER: (crying) I don't want to, Rachel, please . . . please.

RACHEL: Don't want to what? Don't want to go, or you don't want to stay?

MOTHER: I don't want to. You're the cruelest thing that ever lived. Don't you care what happens to me?

RACHEL: After all those sleep-bye pills and chocolate bars and sandwiches and walks, can you ask me that? Yes, I care, but I can't keep you alive. That's not up to me. It never was.

MOTHER: Will I have to sell my furniture? Couldn't I even take my room?

RACHEL: Yes, you can take your room; you can take anything
you like.

The roles, at this point, have reversed; Rachel establishes her
adulthood, but at a heavy cost to her mother's self-image. Calla
sees them off at the bus station, with Rachel telling her, "Calla,
sometimes I wish I could have been different for you." At the
same time that one feels relieved about Rachel's escape, the
viewer is left to ponder what compromises Calla had to make
with herself to continue to live in the stultifying small town.
    We are not allowed to see what happens to Rachel, but when
we leave her on the bus at least we are comforted by the knowledge that she is traveling from one life to another, that she has
acted to improve her situation. On the bus, riding past the familiar
landmarks of the town for the last time, she muses to herself,
"It may always be that my children are temporary, never to
be held. But, so are everyone's. I will be afraid, always. I may
be lonely, always. What will happen? What will happen?" She
has learned that one person cannot hold onto another, that
each individual is responsible for directing his or her own destiny. It is also evident that people cannot relate to their parents
as children all of their lives, nor should parents expect this of
them; at some point, the parent and the child must each recognize the other as an adult, with no right to demand any more
of each other than the adult is willing to give. *Rachel, Rachel*
is a movie of a woman discovering what she must do to survive,
and having the inner fortitude to follow through.
    Renata Adler dubbed *Rachel, Rachel* the "best written,
most seriously acted American movie in a long time."[10] It
garnered four Academy Award nominations, but won none;
Joanne Woodward did win, however, both the New York Film
Critics and Golden Globe awards for Best Actress. The movie
was a critical success, seen as a movie that defied stereotypes
for women, but it made little impression in terms of box office
receipts. One might have reasonably hoped that *Rachel, Rachel*
would be the first of many such filmic explorations of women
and their lives, but such was not the reality.
    Rachel, Rachel did precede two interesting films that dealt
with relationships between elderly fathers and their middle-aged

sons, both suffering through their respective aging problems, *The Arrangement* (1969) and *I Never Sang for my Father* (1970). *The Arrangement* was a slick film from a slick book by Elia Kazan; it chronicled the mid-life crisis of one Eddie Anderson, born Evangelos Topouzogler, the son of a Greek immigrant who had risen to the top of the advertising world but at the cost of his self-respect. Eddie becomes a middle-aged dropout, telling his flabbergasted wife that he wants to "be nothing," and attempting to cope with his ailing father, a sick old man with brain deterioration that has caused extreme paranoia. Eddie's life is a mess, but his "rebirth" after his father's death is equally unconvincing. The movie attempted to deal with issues of aging and goals and life styles, and it failed in a way that *I Never Sang for my Father* did not; *I Never Sang for my Father* deserves closer examination, for it is very similar to *Rachel, Rachel*, but from a male vantage point.

Rachel, Rachel and *I Never Sang for my Father* both raise issues of family responsibility, particularly as they conflict with the desires and needs of the individual. At times, the emotional level of the film is too intense to be believably sustained, but the concerns are genuine and all too real. There are no happy or simple answers to be found here; the opening narration counsels the audience that "Death ends a life, but it does not end a relationship, which struggles on in the survivor's mind, towards some resolution, which it may never find."

Gene Garrison (Gene Hackman) is the son of Tom Garrison (Melvyn Douglas), a former street orphan who managed to rise to civic prominence as mayor and president of the board of education in the town where they lived. The small town figures as prominently as it did in *Rachel, Rachel* as a symbol of oppressive sameness and perpetual adolescence for the children of strong-willed parents. Tom is an opinionated, aggressive old man who no longer has a forum to expound on his beliefs; his contemporaries are all dead, and he is (by his own assessment) "a forgotten man in an ungrateful town." His bitterness consumes a significant portion of his time, brooding about the past rather than living fully in the present. Gene is very devoted to both of his parents, but he wants to move to California to remarry (his first wife having died). His frail mother, Margaret (Dorothy

Stickney), the embodiment of the devoted mother who wants the best for her children, urges Gene to leave. His father warns him however, that "if you go out there to live, it would kill your mother. You are her life. Oh, she's fond of your sister, but you are her life." In all actuality, the move would be devastating to his father, who depends on Gene emotionally for the deference and respect he so needs.

Gene is torn, wanting to leave and have his own life, but feeling obligated to stay. He tries to explain his conflicts to his bed partner: "I get so fed up with being treated like a child by that senile old man. I hate him, and I hate hating him. I hate what it does to me because when I'm around him, somehow I shrink."

The Garrisons have another child, Alice (Estelle Parsons), whom Tom had disowned many years before because she married a Jew. After the mother suffers a fatal heart attack, Alice is the most objective person in the family; her physical removal from the family home had provided her with some measure of perspective that Gene had never acquired. She encourages her father to hire a live-in housekeeper, which he steadfastly refuses to do; she tries to convince Gene to get out while he still can and live his own life. Gene tells Alice (in nicely chauvinistic, patronizing tones) that perhaps it is different between a mother and a daughter, but there exists a special bond between father and son, that the aging man within himself feels for the aged man who is his father. While this emotional bond does, indeed, exist, fathers and sons have no particular monopoly on it. If Gene is trapped by his feelings of obligation, it is within a cage of his own design. He considers placing his father in a nursing home, but he is dissuaded by the tour that shows him old people languishing in wheelchairs, many sedated into passivity, with little to do all day. Gene decides, finally, to go to California; he offers to take his father with him, but Tom stubbornly refuses. Though Tom is the first to lament the boredom and depression he experiences in the town, he will not take the chance of leaving his safe and familiar surroundings. By remaining where he is, Tom retains his position as father; if he went to California, he would lose his status and become a guest, a child in his son's home. Gene leaves, bitterly. Father

and son eventually reconcile enough to visit each other, but Tom
ultimately becomes incapable of living alone, and dies in a
nursing home.

Gene came to the same realization that Rachel had: he could
not, nor was it his responsibility to try to, keep his elderly
parent alive and happy by surrendering his own life to the cause.
Guilt is a man-made, self-imposed feeling which an individual
assumes for himself; Rachel and Gene learned that lesson the
hard way, a lesson their parents had never learned for themselves.

As more Americans live to more advanced ages, more and
more middle-aged children find themselves addressing the problems of responsibility to old parents. It is a situation we may
all face, but it is one we, and the culture, are grossly ill-equipped
to handle at the moment.

Antagonistic mother/son relationships surfaced again in
Where's Poppa? (1970), a Carl Reiner look at family responsibilities. Gordon Hocheiser (George Segal), a lawyer and bachelor,
lives with his crazy, childlike mother whom he takes care of
but really cannot tolerate. His father's dying wish precludes
Mrs. Hocheiser (Ruth Gordon) being placed in an institution,
so Gordon tries to relieve his mounting frustrations by attempting to scare her to death with Gorilla suits and other ridiculous
pranks. Mother, however, is too eccentric to care; she eats
Lucky Charms cereal with Pepsi poured over it, falls asleep at
the dinner table with her face planted firmly in a pile of mashed
potatoes, and keeps asking Gordon where Poppa is, though he
has been dead for several years. She lives in her own world,
where reality seldom intrudes.

Gordon has a difficult time keeping housekeepers, but he
finally finds a woman who is not only a housekeeper, but an
instant object of his passionate love, Louise (Trish Van Devere).
When Gordon invites Louise to have dinner with him and his
mother, Mrs. Hocheiser mortifies Gordon by pulling down his
pants and kissing his rear end, saying she would know it any-
where. Louise runs away in horror. Mrs. Hocheiser, as a character,
is neither lovable nor understandable; she is a collection of all
the worst stereotypes about aging women, and the audience is
driven to extending its collective sympathies to Gordon in his
overwhelming desire to be rid of her.

Louise agrees to marry Gordon if he commits his mother to an institution. He gets his mother to leave the house by telling her they are going on a ride to see Poppa. He goes initially to a ramshackle country establishment called "Gus and Grace's— The Home with a Heart" where seventy-three people are crammed into a firetrap cleverly disguised as a house, attended only by burly Gus. The situation is too horrible for even Gordon, so they move on to "Happy-time Farms," a palatial estate with a strong resemblance to the palace at Versailles. There, Gordon dumps his mother, literally on the door step, and speeds off with Louise to his new motherless life.

The cruelties of *Where's Poppa* are many, offset only by the black comedy of the movie overall; Mrs. Hocheiser's degeneration and abuse occur in a world where all the traditional values are turned upside down. Even considered in a comedic light, however, the implications for the old as useless nuisances to their grown children raise many of the same issues treated more seriously in *Rachel, Rachel* and *I Never Sang for my Father*. As Hollywood entered the seventies, the "me generation" seemed to be gathering momentum, and the individuals destined to suffer the greatest were the elderly, who had been raised with different values and different expectations of familial continuity. It was a situation with no good solution. It was a problem that still needed defining.

NOTES

1. Spoken by character Rachel Cameron in the 1978 Kayos Production, *Rachel, Rachel.*

2. William L. O'Neill, *Coming Apart: An Informal History of America in the 1960s* (New York: Quadrangle/The New York Times Book Co., 1971), p. 199.

3. In a Harris Poll which questioned young people about the "serious" problems of older people, " loneliness" was second only to "not having enough money to live on" as their main expectation of old age. Interestingly enough, while some 60% of the younger respondents anticipated loneliness as a significant problem of the aged, fewer than 15% of elderly people polled on the same issue regarded loneliness as a serious concern. See the August 1975 issue of *Psychology Today* for the complete poll results.

4. *Whatever Happened to Baby Jane?* was the 15th highest money-maker for films released in 1962. See Steinberg, *Reel Facts*, p. 349.

5. Renata Adler, *The New York Times*, 13 June 1968, Section 58, p. 1.

6. Harvey R. Greenberg, *The Movies on Your Mind* (New York: E. P. Dutton and Co., Inc., 1975), pp. 106-137.

7. Ibid., pp. 132-133.

8. Ibid., p. 135.

9. Billboard reproduced in *Mother Goddam, The Story of the Career of Bette Davis*, a biography written by Whitney Stine (New York: Berkley Publishing Corporation, 1974), p. 343.

10. Renata Adler, *The New York Times*, 27 August 1968, Section 36, p. 1.

6

INTIMATIONS OF
REGENERATION(?):
THE OLDER WOMAN
IN THE 1970s AND BEYOND

Is there life after youth?[1]

Hollywood in the seventies had little conception of how to deal with images of women. With so much social unrest about sex roles, filmmakers took the coward's way out and either focused on men's relationships with each other, or on men's brutalization and misuse of women. Taffy Cannon describes the seventies as, "a decade which saw them (women) replaced by crashing automobiles, gushing blood, endless chases, male buddies, high explosives, provocative prepubescence, rampaging animals and a plethora of disasters, both intentional and otherwise."[2]

With the solid, traditional images of women in a state of flux (changes that began in the forties and fifties, but exploded in the seventies), few studios were willing to spend millions of dollars on projects that might generate little public interest and big financial losses. Former movie stars were now older women—Bette Davis, Joan Crawford, Olivia de Havilland—but no scripts utilized the talents of these women in an effort to explore what it meant to be old.

The seventies as a decade did not really exist for women in film until the decade was almost over. The year 1978 saw the release of *Three Women, Welcome to L. A., Looking for Mr. Goodbar, Annie Hall* and *The Goodbye Girl*, among others, ushering in a new awareness of women and their lives. These films placed on screen the new definitions that the culture had grappled with throughout the decade, that a family orientation was not necessarily the only life a woman could rely on for fulfillment, and that every man and woman can be responsible only for themselves, and to themselves. Mothers, who had been under attack since the early sixties, were finally preempted in importance by career women, seeking gratification financially, sexually and emotionally in ways formerly reserved for men. Sexual freedom on the screen became the norm rather than the exception, as the culture became more comfortable with attitudes that seemed distinctly foreign only ten years earlier. A film such as *Rachel, Rachel* would have been only one of many explorations into women and middle-age if it had been made ten years later than it was.

Perhaps one of the most important outcomes of the "me generation" introspection was the beginning of acknowledgement that all of life is a constantly evolving process, with distinct stages correlated to cultural expectations of age. Life is not just three stages of childhood, adulthood, and old age, but a series of complex and interrelated psychological challenges that require recognition. The work of Daniel Levinson, popularized by Gail Sheehy's *Passages*, made the popular culture aware of predictable plateaus and crises of post-adolescent living.

The seventies did, then, see more middle-aged concerns brought to the screen. But what about old age? If the sixties heightened the anxiety people felt about aging, the seventies did not do much to alleviate those fears. Obviously, there were exceptions—which will be discussed momentarily—but the task of reevaluating and establishing new, more positive stereotypes of aging in American film (if it is to happen) belongs to the eighties. The task has already begun with the images of old men, with successful films such as *Harry and Tonto*, *The Sunshine Boys*, *Oh God*, and *Going in Style* finding an audience; it remains to be seen, however, what images older women will reflect in the Hollywood of the future. It is logical that the lives of old men would be examined first; as Cannon points out, "Movies are still made by men about men for men."[3] It is a statement with enough truth in it to be considered part of the reason; one solution to a dearth of older female roles may well be in the encouragement of more women directors and writers, though this obviously does not guarantee a totally satisfactory answer.

The presence, however, of women with well-developed political and social consciences in the production process can make a positive impact. The career of Jane Fonda well illustrates this point. An individual whose movie roles reflect not only her own personal development but also mirror, to some extent, the growth of women's political consciousness during the sixties and seventies: from wide-eyed innocent (*Tall Story*, 1960); to sultry female (*Walk on the Wild Side*, 1962); to every adolescent boy's sexual fantasy (*Barbarella*, 1968); to feminist consciousness *(A Doll's House*, 1973); to political and economic crusader (*Coming Home*, 1978, *The China Syndrome*, 1979 and *Nine to Five*, 1980); and finally, to middle-aged child trying to come to terms with her elderly parents (*On Golden Pond*, 1981); Fonda stands as an example of what can be done with film images when a woman who is determined to express particular points of view manages to gain creative and financial control of the filmmaking process. Fonda has mastered the delicate balance between making a film with a message and making a film that makes money. She is an individual who relies on the power of her messages to affect people's lives, saying "Films, novels and television all play a significant role in slowly altering people's perceptions of themselves and their society. . . . These movies we've made are just pieces in a puzzle."[4] Jessie Bernard, however, is only too accurate when she says that, "Although . . . moving picture audiences tend to include many women . . . cinema for the most part (fails to) reflect female culture accurately, let alone sympathetically."[5]

The problem today is the same as it has been for the entire life of the movie industry; men control the creative, financial and distributive aspects of popular culture entertainment, and thus they give voice to their stories, as well as women's stories, from male perspectives. Bernard comments that "What we do know about the female world from male research is how it impinges on the male world."[6] Consequently, most of what we "know" about older women in movies has been what men thought about women and aging, not necessarily what women

thought about the aging process and its impact on their lives.
The fear we should have at this point is that women like Jane
Fonda, who managed to crack the male wall of control effec-
tively, are the exceptions to the rule.

The seventies did establish some better images of middle-aged
women attempting to debunk the myths of sexual disenfranchisement and uselessness that had plagued the popular consciousness for years—problems that only marriage was thought
to alleviate. Women had always been taught that their adult
lives had to consist primarily of wifehood and motherhood;
eventually, the popular culture began to acknowledge that those
roles were only two possible parts of a more complex whole,
and movies began to capitalize on the new myths being generated
by the women's movement of the seventies. Middle-age continued, certainly, to be a time of potential personal crisis, but
(at least in some major films) more in terms of life choices and
self-direction than falling into line with the status quo. Two films
which amply illustrate some of these changes are *The Turning
Point* (1977) and *An Unmarried Woman*, the first a reexplora-
tion of some of the themes first raised in *All About Eve*, and
the second a portrait of earned self-reliance.

The Turning Point (1977) is a film which tells the story of
two women who chose very different paths to follow in their
youth and who must, in middle age, confront the consequences
of their choices. Dee Dee Rodgers (Shirley MacLaine) and
Emma Jacklin (Anne Bancroft) had been youthful rivals in a
national ballet company. Dee Dee married a fellow dancer and
moved to Oklahoma City, where she and her husband opened
a ballet school for children; their oldest daughter, Emilia, grew
into a very talented dancer. When Emilia is invited to join the
national company, Dee Dee accompanies her to New York City
as a chaperone, returning to the life she had left behind twenty
years earlier.

Emma had chosen to concentrate all her energies on her career;
when we meet her, she is an aging ballerina with virtually no
life off stage, but quickly losing the security of that haven as
younger dancers challenge her position. Both Dee Dee and Emma
are facing new roles; Dee Dee's children are growing and leaving
home, and Emma is no longer the star of the troupe, but an aging

dancer who cannot argue when her own body insists she retire, nor compete with the people who are anxious to take her place. Dee Dee and Emma had each achieved a measure of success, but each is envious of the other. Dee Dee mourns the fame she never achieved and the talent she feels she wasted, and Emma has no real home or family to comfort her now that her professional life is less demanding. Emilia, Emma's godchild, is caught between the two older women; she is talented enough to allow Dee Dee to triumph vicariously through her dancing abilities, and she is vulnerable enough for Emma to assume a maternal role toward her. Dee Dee and Emma finally come to terms with the choices they made so many years before, but not in a spirit of defeat or resignation. Emma does not go out and get married to compensate for lost time, as Margo Channing did in *All About Eve;* nor does Dee Dee reject her life in Oklahoma City to return to New York permanently. Each comes to realize that the quality of life cannot be measured by what one failed to do, but must stand on the tangible aspects of the role they chose. The "turning point" of the title does not just refer to the initial choice of husband or career, but also to the mid-life assessment of the original turning point. Dee Dee and Emma, having recognized the process of their maturation, speak of Emilia and the process she is about to enter:

DEE DEE: Oh, Emma, if only she knew everything we know.

EMMA: It wouldn't matter a damn.

Indeed, one central message of the movie is that a woman can only live her own life; she cannot be directed by outside forces, because ultimately she must be accountable only to herself. Neither woman is destroyed emotionally by the life she failed to lead, but the hope within this film lies in the possibility that young Emilia need not be forced to choose between marriage and her career, but can have both if she so chooses.

An Unmarried Woman (1978) stands as one of the stronger film statements of the late seventies concerning women and their lives. It tells the story of Erica Benton (Jill Clayburgh), who thinks she is happily married—emphasizing the breakdown

of communications between married people—but whose husband,
Martin (Michael Murphy), wants a divorce so that he is free to
marry a twenty-six year old teacher he met while shopping at
Bloomingdale's.

Erica is the type of woman who dabbles in things. She enrolls
in art classes, but does little with her training; she fantasizes
about being a ballet dancer, but does nothing to nurture that
interest. She is an observer—she watches other people live—and
she is not a woman who acts, but who is acted upon. Her married relationship is best characterized by a scene in which she
and Martin are jogging together; Martin steps in a rather large
pile of dog manure, and rants and raves while Erica attempts
to clean his shoe on the grass. Erica takes care of Martin, even
to the point of scraping his shoes.

Martin's desertion (attempting to deal with his own mid-life
crisis) is unexpected and unnerving for Erica; though she does
have the moral support of three close female friends, two of
whom are already divorced and one who is married but cynical
about the relationship. Discussing romance and women and
the manner in which they had been raised, they observe:

FRIEND NO. 1: Bette Davis *always* had self-esteem.

FRIEND NO. 2: Where are all the wonderful women that were
     in the movies in the old days?

FRIEND NO. 3: Where are all the women?

Old-time movie scenarios of love everlasting, regardless of how
many problems arise or how unsuitable individuals become for
each other, just did not exist any longer.

When Martin leaves, Erica (in her own mind) is a victim—*he*
left her, *he* threw her life into turmoil—and she is left behind
to cope with a teenage daughter and a comfortable, familiar
life style that no longer exists. The film chronicles her growth
from a victim to an individual who is capable of living on her
own and handling her own problems. Encouraged by her female
therapist to get back into social circulation, Erica falls in love
with artist Saul (Alan Bates). The audience is aware of the differ-

ences between Erica's marriage and her new involvement because when Saul steps into a pile of dog manure while strolling
with Erica in Soho, he cleans his own shoe!

Martin's girlfriend decides she does not want to marry him,
and when he asks Erica to allow him to return home, she refuses.
Saul wants Erica to spend the summer with him in Vermont,
and she refuses but agrees to visit on holidays. In refusing Saul,
however, she did not do so because she did not love him, but
because she had learned the value of loving herself and the
satisfaction in fulfilling her own needs.

In 1956, Jane Wyman's character, Carrie, in *All That Heaven
Allows*, came to the same point of transition. Carrie, like Erica,
was left floundering by the loss of her husband. The feminine
mystique of the fifties demanded that a new focus had to be
another nurturing relationship, and so Carrie married a man
very different from her first husband and completely reoriented
her life to the new partner, taking on his philosophies and life
style. In *An Unmarried Woman*, Erica's dilemma is quite similar
to Carrie's; Erica is cut adrift from all she held onto as secure
touchstones in her life. The time frame of 1978, however,
sets the stage for a different outcome; Erica finally values herself and her capabilities, and is able to step away from the
socially reinforced need for a woman to be defined by her
relationship to a man. Erica finally sees herself as an individual,
and society is finally able to allow her that viewpoint. It is a
lesson women in film have been struggling to learn for many
years, a lesson that finally seems viable within the popular
culture marketplace.

The last film to be examined is a movie that was originally
released in 1971, but has since become a cult favorite, enjoy-
ing yearly theatre releases in many cities even today. It is a
film that was many years before its time in scope and concern,
and perhaps speaks more to an audience in the 1980s than it
did in 1971. *Harold and Maude* is the story of an emotional
and sexual relationship between an eighteen year old boy,
Harold (Bud Cort) and a seventy-nine year old woman, Maude
(Ruth Gordon).

Harold, the only son of a wealthy mother, spends his time
staging fake suicides and attending funerals of people he does

not know. Maude also attends funerals, which she regularly
departs from in stolen cars to remind people of "here today,
gone tomorrow" and the inadvisability of becoming overly
attached to material possessions. She used to break into pet
stores and liberate canaries at night, because "the world is so
fond of cages." Though never mentioned in the story verbally,
Harold spies a series of numbers tattooed on Maude's forearm,
her concentration camp experiences offered as partial explanation for her eccentric actions and her tremendous concern with
life affirmation. Maude's guiding philosophy is to live life to
the fullest extent, to love and feel and not be concerned with
what people say about it. As she tells Harold, "Everyone has
the right to make an ass out of themselves. You can't let the
world judge you too much."

Maude's concern for a full life also includes a desire for a
planned death, a rational suicide. She has always planned to
kill herself, gently and quietly, on her own terms at the age of
eighty; she does, indeed, follow through on her plans. In 1971,
critic Vincent Canby felt that Maude's suicide invalidated the
overall message to live full lives, "as performers, they both are
so aggressive, so creepy and off-putting, that Harold and Maude
are obviously made for each other, a point the movie itself
refuses to recognize with a twist ending that betrays, I think,
its life-affirming pretensions."[7] In the eighties, however, the effect
of the film is somewhat different; to a culture that wrestled
during the seventies with the moral questions of life-support
systems and the definition of brain death, as well as with an
overall heightened concern for life quality, Maude's action is
not that horrifying. Whereas many people still would not necessarily agree, she would most likely attract a somewhat more
sympathetic appraisal. (But, all things considered, Maude would
not have really concerned herself with whether or not other
people approved of her action.) It is a film that, in 1971, spoke
of future concerns, concerns which, in the 1980s, have finally
arrived to confront the culture head-on.

There is no happy or definitive conclusion for this book,
neither a statement that older women in American films are
now receiving sympathetic and realistic portrayals, nor that
they are doomed to inaccurate and depressing presentations;

the concluding chapter has yet to be lived. It is possible, however, to highlight the changes that have been wrought in two
major areas of concern to aging women and how they are perceived culturally, the older woman as mother and the older woman
as sexual being. It is also possible to speculate on the realistic
possibilities of what future images of aging women in movies
might be.

The social necessity for women to be mothers has undergone
significant revisions in the last fifty years. We have documented
the roles as they changed from the moral necessity and comfort of the thirties, through the cultural imperative of the late
forties and fifties, through the castrating and frightening images
of the sixties, to the beginnings of a cultural acknowledgement
in the seventies that not all women should, or are equipped to,
be mothers. This last stage, however, is still tentative and hardly
yet a serious threat to the mother expectation. The success of
the film *Kramer vs. Kramer*, in which a divorced mother wins
custody of her small child but allows him to stay with her ex-
husband because it is a better situation for both herself and her
son, is encouraging. The mother in the film is not presented
unsympathetically (as she most certainly would have been
several years ago), and the movie offers significant insights into
both parents. So, too, in Neil Simon's *Only When I Laugh*
(1981) do we encounter a middle-aged, alcoholic mother who
has difficulty enough taking care of herself let alone her teenaged daughter, and who agrees to her ex-husband retaining
custody. The mother/daughter divisions of responsibility are
somewhat blurred in this film, allowing the teenager to become
mother to her parent. Marsha Mason's characterization of the
mother tries to tell viewers that parents are not always the
paragons of virtue that we expect them to be, but rather that
they are human beings with human frailties. For every step
forward, however, movies seem to take two steps backwards.
In the well-received and financially successful *Ordinary People*
(1980), Mary Tyler Moore's characterization of Beth is an un-
sympathetic view of a mother who is acting in a decidedly
unmotherly manner. Her favorite son dies in an accident, for
which she blames her surviving son. Beth's sins against motherhood are numerous: she distinguishes between her children and

allows herself to favor one over the other, she refuses to acknowledge the inherent unfairness of her attitude, she is cold and physically removed from her son (denying him the nurturing which is presented as his right), and she refuses to do anything to change her approach. Beth is a woman who is obviously unhappy, and she is trapped in and defined by a world of "sensitive" males (son, husband, son's psychiatrist) who neither understand nor are able to help her cope with the causes of her unrest. The audience is not encouraged to be sympathetic to Beth, who is presented as both cruel and pathetic, and a black eye is bestowed on the woman who fails to fulfill her nurturing functions in an acceptable manner. It is one thing to be inept at mothering; it is quite another matter to be defined by others in relationship to your success (or lack of it) at mothering. Anyone looking for further evidence of the continuation of negative images need only look at one of the most successful movies of 1980, *Friday the 13th*, which features Betsy Palmer as a crazed aging woman, a mother who methodically murders teenaged camp counselors in revenge for the accidental death of her son while attending summer camp many years before. Denied her role as mother by the death of her son, the murderess is unable to go on with her life and becomes, instead, an agent of destruction and death who kills the children of other mothers.

Motherhood, in film and in reality, needs to be finally recognized as only one facet of a woman's life, just as fatherhood is only one facet of a man's life. With a gradual de-mythologizing of maternity as a necessary role for a woman's self-actualization, more attention could be focused on the alternatives available to women. Films in the seventies (many of them financially successful) explored the problems and concerns of middle age. It was a decade in which aging women began to be presented as sexually expressive individuals, causing Marsha McCreadie to comment:

> In 1971 a haggard Cloris Leachman was lavishly grateful for a chance at the young Timothy Bottoms in *The Last Picture Show*, but in 1978 a svelte Lily Tomlin dominates youthful John Travolta in *Moment by Moment*. She holds all the power—the credit

cards, the beach house—as the ads for the film, with her iconographically and sexually 'on top,' remind us.[8]

Movies need to recognize that all of life is a process, that all women are, indeed, aging women (regardless of chronological age). This is not, obviously, a perspective that will be immediately nor wholeheartedly embraced. The presence of mass media insures at least two levels of knowledge, the level of trends and fads which receive media exposure, and the level of people's everyday lives and experiences. The few movies cited here which speak specifically to issues of women and aging are the exceptions in a business which traditionally orients itself to basic common denominators. Hollywood, which made some improvement in these images in the late seventies, finds itself once again besieged in the eighties with a threatened fragmentation of audience by the growth of cable TV, home video and rising costs of movie production. Each Hollywood studio is searching for instant box office success, another *Jaws* or *Raiders of the Lost Ark* to balance the financial statement. Within these realities, new ideas and images which challenge existing stereotypes will be few and far between. Even a film such as *On Golden Pond*, which specifically deals with aging as a central theme, does not really provide new explorations of aging women. Katharine Hepburn's portrayal of Ethel Thayer is firmly in the tradition of nurturing older women so prominent in the thirties and forties; Ethel is strong, assertive, loyal and spunky—in essence, she is the popularly held embodiment of the woman Katharine Hepburn is perceived to be. Ethel has no problems of her own, only problems as they relate to her husband or daughter. The movie, however, struck a responsive chord in the audience which cannot be ignored; the pity is that the film may never have been produced without the sentimental aspect attached to Henry Fonda's and Katharine Hepburn's presence in it, a kind of last hurrah for two long-standing members of Hollywood royalty.

What I have attempted to demonstrate, however, is the undeniable relationship between popular film images and the expression of the social needs of the American culture. As these films have illustrated, the movie theatre can provide more than a place for entertainment; popular movies have the ability to offer tangible articulation and legitimization to cultural concerns and social needs. Film as a public forum allows people, individually and collectively, to examine and incorporate changing information about the world, but at an evolutionary rather than revolutionary pace. There is no reason to believe that movies will cease to function in this particular capacity, or will not continue as agents of both reinforcement and persuasion. The problem, again, is that commercial considerations make it unlikely that we will see the types of images that are broad enough and varied enough to fully examine the many possible dimensions of aging as it affects women. As the postwar baby boom population moves through its life span, the commercial realities of an aging population may well make it profitable for filmmakers to turn their attention more toward the concerns and issues confronting that particular generation. The fragmentation of the video audience by cable may be a blessing in disguise for Hollywood and minority audiences, making it possible to produce products for more narrowly defined audiences and still be able to be cost effective. More women need to be involved in the production of commercial film, but specifically women who are tuned in to female culture and its many dimensions.

In *On Golden Pond*, Jane Fonda portrays a forty-two year old woman who has never been able to make the transition from child to adult in her relationship with her father. She laments the lack of attention she received from him as a child, and is too busy cursing the past to be able to live with the relationship in the present. Tiring of the same list of complaints, Ethel Thayer finally tells her daughter, "All you can do is be disagreeable about the past. What's the point? . . . Life marches by, Chelsea. I suggest you get on with it." Having documented the prevailing themes and images of women and aging in popular film over the past fifty-plus years, it is definitely time to "get on with it;" not to lose sight of the past, but to encourage images which speak to aging women as diverse people rather than stereotypes.

Jessie Bernard says that "some moments in history seem to be more open to change than others."[9] We can only hope that our own era is one of those moments.

NOTES

1. Gail Sheehy, *Passages: Predictable Crises of Adult Life* (New York: Bantam Books, 1974), p. ix.

2. Taffy Cannon, "Women in Love With Film—But Sex Barriers Remain," *Cinegram Magazine*, Summer, 1978, p. 11.

3. Ibid., p. 12.

4. Jane Fonda, quoted by Mike Bygrave and Joan Goodman, "Jane Fonda: Banking On Movie Messages," *American Film*, November, 1981, pp. 38-43.

5. Jessie Bernard, *The Female World* (New York: The Free Press, 1981), p. 458.

6. Ibid., p. 1.

7. Vincent Canby, *The New York Times*, 21 December 1971, Section 51, p. 1.

8. Marsha McCreadie, "Women: The Images," *American Film*, December 1979, pp. 31, 63.

9. Bernard, *The Female World*, p. 554.

BIBLIOGRAPHY

Adler, Renata. Review of *Rachel, Rachel. The New York Times*, 27
    August 1968, Section 36, p. 1.
——. Review of *Rosemary's Baby. The New York Times*, 13 June 1968,
    Section 58, p. 1.
Baxandall, Rosalyn et al. *America's Working Women*. New York: Vintage
    Books, 1976.
Beauvoir, Simone de. *The Second Sex*. New York: Bantam Books, 1968
    (12th Edition).
Berger, Peter L. and Thomas Luckmann. *The Social Construction of
    Reality*. Garden City, New York: Doubleday-Anchor, 1967.
Bergman, Andrew. *We're in the Money: Depression America and Its Films*.
    New York: Harper Colophon Books, 1971.
Bernard, Jessie. *The Female World*. New York: The Free Press, 1981.
——.*The Future of Motherhood*. New York: The Dial Press, 1974.
——. *Women, Wives, Mothers: Values and Options*. Chicago: Aldine
    Publishing Company, 1975.
Brooks, Tim and Earle Marsh. *The Complete Directory to Prime Time
    Network TV Shows, 1946-Present*. New York: Ballantine Books, 1979.
Bygrave, Mike and Joan Goodman. "Jane Fonda: Banking On Movie
    Messages." *American Film*, November 1981, pp. 38-43.
Canby, Vincent. Review of *Harold and Maude. The New York Times*,
    21 December 1971, Section 51, p. 1.
Cannon, Taffy. "Women In Love With Film—But Sex Barriers Remain."
    Cinegram Magazine, Summer 1978, pp. 11-14.
Cawelti, John. *Adventure, Mystery and Romance*. Chicago: The University
    of Chicago Press, 1976.
——. *The Six-Gun Mystique*, Bowling Green, Ohio: Bowling Green Uni-
    versity Popular Press, n. d.

Cripps, Thomas. *Slow Fade to Black: The Negro in American Film,
     1900-1942.* New York: Oxford University Press, 1977.
Crowther, Bosley, Review of *High Sierra. The New York Times,* 2 May 1941,
     p. 25.
Daly, Mary. *Gyn/Ecology: The Metaethics of Radical Feminism.* Boston:
     Beacon Press, 1978.
Deckard, Barbara. *The Women's Movement.* New York: Harper and Row,
     1975.
Degler, Carl N. *At Odds: Women and the Family in America from the
     Revolution to the Present.* New York: Oxford University Press, 1980.
Douglas, Ann. *The Feminization of American Culture.* New York: Avon
     Books, 1977.
Duncan, Hugh Dalziel. *Communication and Social Order.* London: Oxford
     University Press, 1962.
Edmondson, Madeline and David Rounds. *From Mary Noble to Mary
     Hartman: The Complete Soap Opera Book.* New York: Stein and
     Day, 1976.
Ehrenreich, Barbara and Deirdre English. *For Her Own Good: 150 Years
     of the Experts' Advice to Women.* Garden City, New York:
     Doubleday-Anchor, 1979.
Filene, Peter Gabriel. *Him/Her/Self: Sex Roles in Modern America:*
     New York: The New American Library, Inc., 1976.
Forster, E. M. *Aspects of the Novel.* New York: Harcourt, Brace and
     World, Inc., 1927.
French, Brandon. *On the Verge of Revolt: Women in American Films
     of the Fifties.* New York: Frederick Ungar Publishing Company, 1978.
Goodman, Paul and Frank O. Gatell. *America in the Twenties: The
     Beginnings of Contemporary America.* New York: Holt, Rinehart
     and Winston, Inc., 1972.
Greenberg, Harvey R., M. D. *The Movies on Your Mind.* New York: E. P.
     Dutton and Company, Inc., 1975.
Hall, Ben M. *The Best Remaining Seats: The Golden Age of the Movie
     Palace.* New York: Bramhall House, 1961.
Halliwell, Leslie. *The Filmgoer's Companion.* 4th ed. New York: Avon
     Books, 1975.
Haskell, Molly. *From Reverence to Rape: The Treatment of Women in
     the Movies.* New York: Holt, Rinehart and Winston, 1973.
Janeway, Elizabeth. *Between Myth and Morning: Women Awakening.*
     New York: William Morrow and Company, Inc., 1975.
——. *Man's World, Woman's Place: A Study in Social Mythology.* New
     York: Dell Publishing Company, Inc., 1971.
Jowett, Garth. *Film: The Democratic Art.* Boston: Little, Brown and
     Company, 1976.

Lerner, Gerda. *The Majority Finds its Past: Placing Women in History.*
New York: Oxford University Press, 1979.

Littlefield, Henry M. "The Wizard of Oz: Parable On Populism." *American Quarterly,* XVI, Spring, 1964, pp. 47-58.

Lundberg, Ferdinand and Marynia Farnham. *Modern Woman: The Lost Sex.* New York: 1947.

Mayer, Allan J. et al. "The Graying of America." *Newsweek,* 28 February 1977, pp. 50-65.

McCreadie, Marsha. "Women: The Images." *American Film,* December, 1979, pp. 31, 63.

Mellon, Joan. *Women and Their Sexuality in the New Film.* New York: Dell Publishing Comapny, 1973.

Moore, Raylyn. *Wonderful Wizard, Marvelous Land.* Bowling Green, Ohio: Bowling Green University Popular Press, 1974.

Morgan, Marabel. *The Total Woman.* New York: Pocket Books, 1975.

Nye, Russel. *The Unembarrassed Muse: The Popular Arts in America.* New York: The Dial Press, 1970.

O'Neill, William L. *Coming Apart: An Informal History of America in the 1960's.* New York: Quadrangle-The New York Times Book Company, 1971.

Partnow, Elaine, ed. *The Quotable Woman.* New York: Anchor Books, 1978.

Powdermaker, Hortense. *Hollywood: The Dream Factory.* New York: The Universal Library, 1950.

Review of *Sunset Boulevard. The New York Times,* 11 August 1950, Section 15, p. 2.

Rich, Adrienne. *Of Woman Born: Motherhood as Experience and Institution.* New York: W. W. Norton & Company, 1976.

Rollin, Betty. "Motherhood: Who Needs It?" *Look Magazine,* 22 September 1970, pp. 15-17.

Rosen, Marjorie. *Popcorn Venus: Women, Movies and the American Dream.* New York: Avon Books, 1973.

Rothman, Sheila M. *Woman's Proper Place: A History of Changing Ideals and Practices, 1870 to the Present.* New York: Basic Books, Inc., 1978.

Rupp, Leila J. *Mobilizing Women for War: German and American Propaganda, 1939-1945.* Princeton, New Jersey: Princeton University Press, 1978.

Sebald, Hans. *Momism: The Silent Disease of America.* Chicago: Nelson Hall, 1976.

Sheehy, Gail. *Passages: Predictable Crises of Adult Life.* New York: Bantam Books, 1974.

Slater, Philip E. *The Pursuit of Loneliness.* Boston: Beacon Press, 1970.

Sontag, Susan. "The Double Standard of Aging." In *No Longer Young:*

The Older Woman in America. Ann Arbor, Michigan: The Institute
of Gerontology, The University of Michigan, 1975.

Spock, Benjamin, M. D. *The Common Sense Book of Baby and Child Care.*
New York: Duell, Sloan and Pearce, 1946.

Steinberg, Cobbett. *Reel Facts: The Movie Book of Records.* New York:
Vintage Books, 1978.

Stine, Whitney. *Mother Goddamn: The Story of the Career of Bette Davis.*
New York: Berkley Publishing Corporation, 1974.

Wallechinsky, David and Irving Wallace. *The People's Almanac.* Garden
City, New York: Doubleday and Company, 1975.

Walsh, Andrea. "Films of Suspicion and Distrust: Undercurrents of Female
Consciousness in the 1940s." *Film and History,* February, 1978, pp. 1-8.

Weibel, Kathryn. *Mirror, Mirror: Images of Women Reflected in Popular
Culture.* Garden City, New York: Anchor Press, 1977.

Weiss, Nancy Pottishman. "Mother, The Invention of Necessity: Dr.
Benjamin Spock's *Baby and Child Care.*" *American Quarterly,* XXIX,
Winter, 1977, pp. 519-546.

Williams, Juanita H. *Psychology of Women: Behavior in a Biosocial
Context.* New York: W. W. Norton and Company, Inc., 1977.

Wood, Michael. *America in the Movies.* New York: Basic Books, Inc., 1975.

Wylie, Philip. *Generation of Vipers.* New York: Farrar and Rinehart, Inc.,
1942.

Zinman, David. *Saturday Afternoon at the Bijou.* New York: Castle Books,
1973.

FILMS
CITED

The following annotated filmography includes the films mentioned specifically within the text. Ordered alphabetically by film title, each entry contains the following progression of information: title, director, studio, year, and principal actors/actresses.

Affair to Remember, An. Leo McCarey, Twentieth-Century Fox, 1957. Cary Grant, Deborah Kerr, Cathleen Nesbitt.

Melodrama which underscores the close connection between a woman's "true" fulfillment and her role as nurturer.

All About Eve. Joseph L. Mankiewicz, Twentieth-Century Fox, 1950. Bette Davis, Anne Baxter, Celeste Holm.

Bette Davis suffers a mid-life crisis in choosing between her career and marriage: marriage wins.

All That Heaven Allows. Douglas Sirk, Universal, 1956. Jane Wyman, Rock Hudson, Agnes Moorehead.

Interesting film because it sanctions an older woman/younger man romance and marriage, though it definitely contends that a woman is only whole as a wife.

Anniversary, The. Roy Ward Baker, Seven Arts-Hammer Productions, 1968. Bette Davis.

Bette Davis as the tyrannical mother of a strange assortment of sons, each of whom would like to eliminate her. Black Comedy.

Arrangement, The. Elia Kazan, Warner Brothers-Seven Arts, 1969. Kirk Douglas, Deborah Kerr, Faye Dunaway.

> Kirk Douglas as an advertising whiz who finds himself successful but miserable; attempts to make peace between himself and the compromises he has made in the past.

Awful Truth, The. Leo McCarey, Columbia, 1937. Irene Dunne, Cary Grant, Cecil Cunningham.

> Comedy about marriage and divorce. Notable for Cecil Cunningham, who portrays a middle-aged woman who appears chic and happy, but actually regrets her single life and attempts to keep her niece from the same fate.

Back Street. John M. Stahl, Universal, 1932. Irene Dunne, Jane Darwell.

> A melodrama depicting the waste of a human life, as Irene Dunne portrays the life-long mistress of a married man.

Bordertown. Archie Mayo, Warner Brothers, 1934. Paul Muni, Bette Davis, Soledad Jimenez.

> Drama about an impoverished Mexican who yearns for the life money and power can provide; ultimately frustrated in his attempt to break out of the barrio.

Citizen Kane. Orson Welles, RKO, 1941. Orson Welles, Joseph Cotton, Agnes Moorehead.

> The classic story of the rise and fall of a powerful, wealthy man. Interesting for the relationship between the main character and his mother.

Come Fill the Cup. Gordon Douglas, Warner Brothers, 1951. James Cagney, Gig Young.

> Ex-alcoholic Cagney character attempts to save alcoholic Gig Young character, who is afflicted not only with a drinking problem, but a mother problem as well.

Condemned Women. Lew Landers, RKO, 1938. Esther Dale.

> Drama depicting the conditions within a women's prison; Esther Dale portrays a tough, totally unfeminine matron.

Criminal Code, The. Howard Hawks, Columbia, 1930. Walter Huston, Ethel Wales.

> Primarily prison film; contains slight sub-plot about the effect of prison life on people who work within the structure but are not criminals, particularly one female secretary/housekeeper.

Each Dawn I Die. William Keighley, Warner Brothers, 1939. James Cagney, George Raft, Emma Dunn.

> The story of two men, one a criminal and the other a crusading reporter, and the effect their family ties had on their adult lives.

Easy Living. Mitchel Leisen, Paramount, 1937. Jean Arthur, Ray Milland, Esther Dale, Mary Nash.

> Comedy which, like many other Depression era films, depicts the rich as silly and frivolous and the less well-to-do as somewhat more noble stock.

Egg and I, The. Chester Erskine, Universal-International, 1947. Claudette Colbert, Fred MacMurray, Ida Moore.

> Idealistic city dwellers decide to return to the simple life in the country to raise chickens. Film contains a number of interesting portrayals of older women.

Female on the Beach. Joseph Pevney, Universal, 1955. Joan Crawford, Jeff Chandler.

> Joan Crawford as a tough but lonely widow; Jeff Chandler as a gigolo with a rampant case of Momism.

Friday the 13th. Sean S. Cunningham, Paramount Pictures, 1980. Betsy Palmer, Adrienne King, Harry Crosby.

> A brutally graphic excuse for violence, cleverly disguised as a horror film, with Betsy Palmer as a deranged older woman who systematically kills a group of teen-aged camp counselors.

Gold Diggers of 1933. Mervyn LeRoy, Warner Brothers, 1933. Joan Blondell, Ruby Keeler, Dick Powell, Aline MacMahon.

> Musical depicting the man-chasing antics of unmarried women.

Gold Diggers of 1935. Busby Berkeley. Warner Brothers, 1934. Dick
  Powell, Alice Brady.

  Musical set in a resort for the wealthy. Contains a particularly telling
  portrayal of a wealthy older woman in the Alice Brady character.

Grapes of Wrath, The. John Ford, Twentieth-Century Fox, 1940. Henry
  Fonda, Jane Darwell.

  The trials of the Joads, an Okie farm family led by the spirit and
  courage of the indomitable Ma Joad.

Harold and Maude. Hal Ashby, Paramount, 1971. Ruth Gordon, Bud Cort.

  An unusual comedy with heavy doses of life affirmation; Gordon
  as Maude is a character for whom time and age mean little—she is
  one of the original free spirits.

Harriet Craig. Vincent Sherman, Columbia, 1950. Joan Crawford, Wendall
  Corey.

  Crawford as a manipulative shrew who gets exactly what she deserves
  in the end. Interesting for its very obvious model of what constitutes
  a "good" wife.

High Sierra. Raoul Walsh, Warner Brothers, 1941. Humphrey Bogart, Ida
  Lupino.

  Bogart as a criminal with a heart of gold, whose better nature is
  revealed in his relationship with an elderly couple whom he befriends.

Hush, Hush Sweet Charlotte. Robert Aldrich, Twentieth-Century Fox, 1964.
  Bette Davis, Olivia de Havilland.

  Images of degeneration and decay on a Southern plantation, with
  Bette Davis as the noble but long-suffering victim.

I am a Fugitive from a Chain Gang. Mervyn LeRoy, Warner Brothers,
  1932. Paul Muni.

  One of the few Depression era films to direct itself to social problems,
  depicting a normless society that crushes the individual.

I Never Sang for my Father. Gilbert Cates, Columbia, 1970. Gene Hackman,
  Melvyn Douglas, Estelle Parsons.

Interesting examination of the stress which often occurs in relationships between older parents and their grown children.

Inside Daisy Clover. Robert Mulligan, Warner Brothers, 1965. Ruth Gordon, Natalie Wood.

Improbable rags-to-riches story that presents a mother/daughter relationship in which the two women have reversed roles psychologically.

Jezebel. William Wyler, Warner Brothers, 1938. Bette Davis, Henry Fonda, Faye Bainter.

Davis' compelling portrait of a spoiled Southern belle who finally finds redemption in self-sacrifice.

Joy of Living. Tay Garnett, RKO, 1936. Irene Dunne, Douglas Fairbanks, Jr., Alice Brady.

Dunne as successful Broadway star supporting a parasitic and ungrateful family, especially the mother character played by Brady.

Kramer vs. Kramer. Robert Benton, Columbia, 1980. Dustin Hoffman, Meryl Streep, Jane Alexander.

A contemporary look at marriage, divorce, and custody rights; reeks with sensitivity, but manages to suggest that not every woman needs motherhood for self-fulfillment.

Lady for a Day. Frank Capra, Columbia, 1933. May Robson, Guy Kibbee.

Capra's version of the Cinderella story, adapted from a Damon Runyon story. Depicts the transformation of aging Apple Annie into a society matron. Capra later remade this as *Pocketful of Miracles*, with Bette Davis in the lead role.

Little Ceasar. Mervyn Douglas, First National, 1930. Edward G. Robinson, Douglas Fairbanks, Jr.

Gangster movie; interesting for its portrayal of immigrant mothers.

Little Minister, The. Richard Wallace, RKO, 1934. Katharine Hepburn, Beryl Mercer.

The story of an innocent country minister and the mysterious girl he falls in love with; Beryl Mercer plays the minister's devoted mother.

Lost Moment, The. Martin Gabel, Universal, 1947. Robert Cummings, Susan Hayward, Agnes Moorehead.

Based on Henry James' *The Aspern Papers*; particularly interesting for Moorehead's portrayal of a 105 year old woman.

Miracle Woman, The. Frank Capra, Columbia, 1931. Barbara Stanwyck, Beryl Mercer.

Stanwyck as a dishonest evangelist who is led to emotional salvation by the simple and honest example of Mercer's character.

My Man Godfrey. Gregory La Cava, Universal, 1936. William Powell, Carole Lombard, Alice Brady.

Screwball comedy with Brady as the archetypal society matron who possesses a head stuffed with feathers.

Mother Carey's Chickens. Rowland V. Lee, C & C Films, 1938. Ruby Keeler, Fay Bainter, Margaret Hamilton.

Inspiring drama about a widow and her children, who are determined to keep their family intact despite large obstacles.

None but the Lonely Heart. Clifford Odets, RKO, 1944. Cary Grant, Ethel Barrymore.

Story of a tempestuous relationship between a mother and son. Barrymore's performance won an Academy Award.

On Golden Pond. Mark Rydell, IPC Films, 1981. Katharine Hepburn, Henry Fonda, Jane Fonda.

Screen version of Ernest Thompson's play, concerning an aging professor who is afraid of death, his fiercely loyal and protective wife, and their middle-aged daughter who is trying desperately to grow up.

Only When I Laugh. Glenn Jordon, Columbia Pictures, 1981. Marsha Mason, Kristy McNichol.

Neil Simon's look at the dynamics of the mother/daughter relationship when the roles are reversed.

Ordinary People. Robert Redford, Paramount Pictures, 1980. Donald Sutherland, Mary Tyler Moore, Timothy Hutton.

Alienation and communication breakdown within a rapidly dis-integrating upper class family.

Pocketful of Miracles. Frank Capra, Franton Productions, 1961. Bette Davis, Ann-Margaret, Glenn Ford.

Remake of *Lady for a Day*, starring Davis as Apple Annie. Film marked Ann-Margaret's screen debut.

Psycho. Alfred Hitchcock, Paramount, 1960. Anthony Perkins, Janet Leigh.

Though generally remembered for its grisly shower scene, this film documents what is perhaps the worse case of Momism to ever appear on the screen.

Public Enemy. William A. Wellman, Warner Brothers, 1931. James Cagney, Beryl Mercer.

A gangster movie with Cain-and-Abel overtones; Mercer is the long-suffering mother caught in the middle.

Rachel, Rachel. Paul Newman, Kayos Productions, 1968. Joanne Wood-ward, Geraldine Fitzgerald, Estelle Parsons.

A film which depicts the sexual and psychological awakening of a middle-aged school teacher who has always lived with her mother. The film also explores the complex relationship between mother and daughter.

Roberta. William A. Seiter, RKO, 1935. Irene Dunne, Randolph Scott, Helen Westley, Fred Astaire.

Westley as an aging dress designer who is wealthy but ever mindful of her humble beginnings. More a vehicle for Dunne as the talented protege.

Rosemary's Baby. Roman Polanski, Paramount, 1968. Ruth Gordon, Mia Farrow.

Modern day gothic tale of devil worshippers and demonic impreg-nation, with Ruth Gordon as the eccentric neighbor.

Rosie. David Lowell Rich, Universal, 1967. Rosalind Russell, Sandra Dee, Audrey Meadows, Margaret Hamilton.

Russell as an elderly millionaire who defies the notion of age-appropriate behavior but must fight for her right to act as she pleases. This is primarily a comedy, but with serious overtones.

Sergeant York. Howard Hawks, Warner Brothers, 1941. Gary Cooper, Margaret Wycherly.

The story of a World War I hero, whose devotion to his mother is a very touching element in his life.

Smartest Girl in Town. Joseph Santley, RKO, 1936. Ann Sothern, Helen Broderick.

Sothern as a young woman determined to marry a rich man, and willing to go to great lengths to do it. Comedy.

Snake Pit, The. Anatole Litvak, Twentieth-Century Fox, 1948. Olivia de Havilland.

Grim but effective exploration of mental illness and institutions, as well as what constitutes a "proper role" for an adult woman.

Sunset Boulevard. Billy Wilder, Paramount, 1950. Gloria Swanson, William Holden.

The pathetic story of an aging movie queen who cannot accept the fact that her youth, and her career, are long gone.

There Goes the Groom. Joseph Santley, RKO, 1937. Ann Sothern, Burgess Meredith.

Comedy reigns as a once-wealthy family tries to regain its financial footing by marrying one of the daughters to a wealthy but innocent man. Another instance of a scatterbrained mother.

Too Hot to Handle. Herman Shumlin, Warner Brothers, 1938. Clark Gable, Myrna Loy, Marjorie Main.

Reporters for newsreel companies try to outrace each other for stories. Main as a tough and cynical, but lovable secretary, who can handle anything.

Turning Point, The. Herbert Ross, Twentieth-Century Fox, 1977. Shirley MacLaine, Anne Bancroft.

The story of two women, each of whom chooses a different path to follow, and each of whom must face the consequences of those choices in mid-life.

Unmarried Woman, An. Paul Mazursky, Twentieth-Century Fox, 1978. Jill Clayburgh, Michael Murphy.

The Clayburgh character thinks she has the perfect life. The movie chronicles what happens when that familiar life explodes, and what a middle-aged woman faces as she constructs a new reality on her own terms.

Watch on the Rhine. Herman Shumlin, Warner Brothers, 1943. Bette Davis, Paul Lukas, Lucile Watson.

Hard-hitting adaptation of Lillian Hellman's play, with Davis as the wife of an underground anti-Nazi leader and Watson as the strong and feisty matriarch of a powerful and wealthy American family.

Whatever Happened to Baby Jane? Robert Aldrich, Warner Brothers, 1962. Bette Davis, Joan Crawford.

Davis and Crawford as aging sisters who live their lives through the bitterness of the past. Frightening portrait of what people are capable of doing to each other.

Where's Poppa? Carl Reiner, United Artists, 1970. George Segal, Ruth Gordon, Trish VanDevere.

Eccentric comedy recounting the efforts of a son to rid himself of the burden of caring for his senile mother.

Wild in the Streets. Barry Shear, American International, 1968. Shelley Winters, Christopher Jones.

Futuristic look at an America run by a rock star who suffers from Momism and ageism. Shelley Winters is superb as the cloying, suffocating mother.

Wizard of Oz, The. Victor Fleming, MGM, 1939. Judy Garland et al., Clara Blandick.

No explanation necessary!

Wolf Man, The. George Wagner, Universal, 1941. Lon Chaney Jr., Maria Ouspenskaya.

The story of the legend of the werewolf, with Maria Ouspenskaya as the wise old gypsy woman.

You Can't Take It With You. Frank Capra, Columbia, 1938. Jean Arthur, Lionel Barrymore.

A movie whose message is clear—true wealth is not found in money, but in the love of your family.

Young Mr. Lincoln. John Ford, Twentieth-Century Fox, 1939. Henry Fonda, Alice Brady, Marjorie Weaver.

The story of an isolated incident in the early legal career of Abraham Lincoln, where he defends two innocent boys and the rights of American motherhood.

INDEX

About the Author

KAREN M. STODDARD is Assistant Professor and Chairperson of the Communication Arts Department at the College of Notre Dame in Baltimore. She received her Ph.D. in American Studies from the University of Maryland. She has written articles for *The Journal of Popular Film and Television*, *American Women Writers*, and *Currents of Warm Life*.